LOVE
HARDER

LOVE
HARDER

Pamela Williams

CITI OF
BOOKS

CITIOFBOOKS, INC.
3736 Eubank NE Suite A1
Albuquerque, NM 87111-3579
www.citiofbooks.com
Hotline: 1 (877) 389-2759
Fax: 1 (505) 930-7244

Ordering Information:

Quantity sales. Special discounts are available on quantity purchases by corporations, associations, and others. For details, contact the publisher at the address above.

Printed in the United States of America.

ISBN-13:   Softcover   978-1-963209-25-9
              Ebook   978-1-963209-27-3
              Softcover   978-1-963209-26-6

Library of Congress Control Number: 2024900611

Table Of Contents

"LOVE HARDER"

FOREWORD

We are called to love. That is no mistake. In fact, it is our greatest Word in the Bible. To love God and love one another. Love is the most powerful emotion and that is no mistake.in fact it is our greatest Word/Command in the Bible. Love has the power to transform each of us. No matter what our situation, love can alter the course of our earthly journey.

Our very being was created from the greatest love. The love of God. That being said, how many of us manage to mess up love so much? Love can be difficult to find. It is easy to lose. Why do many seem void of it? The answer to messed-up love is Sin.

We are all sinners in need of help. We cannot go it alone and cannot free ourselves from our sin condition. Sin hurts us and kills us. Finding yourself is easier said than done. We've all done things we're not proud of or wished our actions led to different outcomes. Whatever the situation, figuring out how to forgive yourself is key to unraveling your past and moving forward.

Romans 6:23

Jesus Christ delivers those who trust him from the treadmill of sin and condemnation (death) as He grants us the free gift of fellowship, Hope, and purpose right now and in the age to come (eternal life).

To make things even more complicated, forgiveness, even of oneself, doesn't happen overnight. "Remind yourself that everyone makes mistakes and it's okay to have feelings such as guilt or shame," Take care of yourself, both physically and mentally, as forgiving yourself won't happen overnight and may take much time.

The biggest obstacle to self-forgiveness is our tendency to wallow in our guilt. It's not just because we know we've done something wrong;

everyone does that. But some of us actually draw those bad feelings around ourselves like a warm kitten.

We curl up in a ball and say, "Hey! Look how bad I feel! See how I'm suffering! I'm pitiful! I'm pathetic! I can't be punished any more than this."

It's a "form of penance." Instead of taking responsibility for what we've done by trying to repair the damage or make things right, many of us unconsciously decide to punish ourselves by feeling miserable for the rest of our lives.

Misery does love company. If you keep beating yourself up, then a person who tries to love you is going to get beat up, too. It's inevitable. Anyone who's wallowing in guilt is going to be more withdrawn, more critical, and less open than normal.

Our mind affects our body in a zillion interconnecting ways, and those guilty feelings you're nurturing are generating chemicals that are headed straight for your vital organs. It's no wonder that studies on forgiveness have led scientists to suspect that those who have difficulty forgiving are more likely to experience heart attacks, high blood pressure, depression, and other ills.

Forgiveness is a tool with which we face what we've done in the past, acknowledge our mistakes, and move on. It does not mean that you condone or excuse what happened. It does not mean that you forget, and it doesn't mean you stop talking about it. Being open, honest, and communicable about it helps you and others learn and grow through trauma experiences.

There's a season for our suffering and regret. We have to have that. But the season ends; the world moves on. And we need to move on too.

Some people find self-forgiveness hard because they are trapped in their suffering and feelings of remorse.

What to do when I can't forgive myself?

*Seek God…
*Acknowledge your mistake out loud. …
*Think of each mistake as a learning experience. …

*Give yourself permission to put this process on hold. ...
*Have a conversation with your inner critic. ...
*Notice when you are being self-critical. ...
*Quiet the negative messages of your inner critic.

The best way to forgive oneself is by practicing self-love. Think kind thoughts about yourself and show yourself some compassion. You are more than your past mistakes.

Ways one can begin self-forgiveness.

*Responsibility: Accept what has happened and show yourself compassion. *Remorse: Use guilt and remorse as a gateway to positive behavior change. *Restoration: Make amends with whomever you're forgiving, even if it's yourself. *Renewal: Learn from experience and grow as a person.

1 Corinthians 13:4-5.

As the failure to forgive ourselves hinders our love of others, so our love for others can facilitate self-forgiveness.

The Bible points toward one sin that can't be forgiven on God's list and that is the sin of rejecting Him and refusing His offer of forgiveness and a new life in Jesus Christ. This alone is the unforgivable sin, because it means we are saying that the Holy Spirit's witness about Jesus is a lie.

Perhaps the biggest reason self-forgiveness is difficult is inherent to the process itself. To process our experiences, we must become present in our suffering. Making it harder is the fact that our brain remembers. We cannot forget. To tell someone to do so is folly.

Forgiveness, whether of someone else or yourself, can mean you accept actions and behaviors that occurred while willing to move forward and away from your past sins. Forgiving yourself may mean letting go of the feelings and emotions associated with what went wrong.

The act of forgiveness delivers tangible, structural changes in the brain and body as neural networks that control stress, pain, and awareness and processes that increase stress hormones in the body and negatively impact physical and mental health are dialed down.

The hardest part of forgiving is forgetting because we cannot remove the past from our brains.

1 Corinthians 5:21.

For our sake he made him to be sin who knew no sin, so that in him we might become the righteousness of God.

When you attempt to punish yourself or atone for your sins with self-condemnation you diminish Christ's atonement on your behalf

The greatest gift we are given is love. It is also the greatest gift we can ever receive. Our job is to live a life of love and give it to others.

God's love poured out on us covers our sins. That is no accident. He seeks us out to love us, with a love like no other. Love Himself is God. Speak the name and He is.

Our one true love and teacher of love.

DEDICATION

This book was written and is dedicated to James who frequently challenged me regarding my lack of love for "some" people. His concern came as an insightful and highly impactful challenge that led me on a journey of forgiveness accompanied by many apologies.

I was asked by James one day how well I got along with my friends and neighbors. Then he questioned how much I loved each of them and what that looked like to me. James was legitimately concerned about my ability to love, and he cared enough about my journey to point out an obvious and embarrassing flaw of mine. I did not love most people "enough", I loved some people a little and others, not so much. Lots of people I regularly have contact with I don't think about much at all.

You see, I fall into the category of "sinner." I can't help but love myself, more than anyone else. We love to love ourselves and put ourselves above others, including God. We also love our sin. This is the infection of sin, that we all suffer from.

I am not a theologian. I'm a layperson trying to stumble through a life, looking to the Heavens for my Savior Jesus. I speak with no authority but with curiosity and wonder at God's love of this sinful being. I would refer to myself as an advanced beginner seeking to know God.

In Lutheranism, there is "law and gospel. "With this in mind, this "sin" condition is far less acceptable than what God asks from each of us. I have needed to develop a love strategy and in truth adopt one that could take the place of my blasé attitude. Then begin the hard work of loving people "harder".

As I began working even harder on this topic and taking it to another level, it became even more evident and it was brought to my attention by James that in fact, I did not even allow people to love me. It took some time to mull over that statement and take it in.

That was difficult to digest but ultimately after thoughtful consideration and a big dose of honesty, I eventually and sadly agreed that James was accurate. He had a pretty good handle on who I was. I did distance myself from others and had a wall up that kept love at bay.

I really had to begin the process of unraveling that scenario and understand where and when it originated. I needed to change the narrative because as an adult I can reprogram trauma responses. They are no longer useful to me. They are damaging as I sojourn through life.

I've gone through this life rejecting many people and keeping others at a comfortable distance. I rarely considered God's greatest Words to love Him and others as I am loved by God. I don't even like most people let alone love everyone.

I am even on occasion rude to people, especially strangers and service workers. I try not to be difficult and rude, but the behavior is painfully and deeply ingrained in my heart. My heart doesn't always feel safe. As a child, I needed to be guarded, so I adopted defensive measures for protection. What I needed to do in my childhood is no longer necessary as I'm capable of taking care of myself now.

I sometimes can avoid the problem of "being rude" by just walking away or hanging up the phone on people. In my feeble excuse of defense, I must explain that most of the people I hang up on are not particularly helpful or are rude themselves. I do not care to engage with difficult people or exasperating situations. I'm enough of a handful and frequently try to lessen the opportunity to cause or be trouble by just disengaging.

Another communication issue I have is not being heard during a conversation. It's a trauma trigger for me. I can shut down emotionally and become catatonic and or throw up in response to being ignored or dismissed. It happens by force of habit, and it happens frequently when it does occur, I need to retrain in order to begin calming myself down. I need a time-out.

Fighting and loud arguing and yelling at me are another significant trigger. I stop interacting altogether, become catatonic, and need to go to bed or find a quiet safe place to wait it out and try to go to sleep. Sleep is a certain cure. I must fall asleep to stop my nervous system from overreacting. When I wake up the panic and anxiety I felt is resolved and I can breathe again. Trying to fight through all that anxiety takes an emotional toll.

Though I haven't yet experienced death, it feels very much how I imagine it. Funny how we say we feel like we're dying in stressful situations, but we have no legitimate reference point for it.

If there is hostility and/or violence during a disagreement, it will frequently land me in the hospital. I cannot even watch people being mean to each other on television because it physically hurts me.

As a result of my own personal undesirable and inconsistent behavior, I've now become a walking apology. I am not successfully loving others according to God's command try as I may, I'm failing at love which requires intentional change and work on my part with God's help. I cannot possibly begin to bridge that imperfect divide without God.

I wrote this book as a response to the predicament I find myself in, of loving many people "less" and being intentional about who I give more or less love to. I'm a broken, imperfect, and emotionally handicapped human. I'm being cajoled and encouraged to pay more attention to how I love and to change my heart and behavior towards others. This is a huge task which I'm capable of failing miserably. I'm actively working on the problem with God's help. I have to intentionally and daily pick up that cross, to live God's great "love" command.

I'm not required to be in a relationship with everyone I encounter or agree with everything people say and I don't even have to like certain people, but I do have to love them.

The strength, knowledge, and power needed to create necessary change in me are directed and provided. On my own, I cannot accomplish any significant changes. I admit I'm a sinner to the core and I need help, especially with loving people harder.

I will continue to sin every day of my life because that is my nature, but I can use my awareness to improve my sinful nature with God's help and guidance through His Living Word.

Jesus' Love for Us

How much does Jesus love me? We all want to be in a relationship with someone who loves us very much. None of us sign up for relationship failures or divorce. Our friendships while not romantic relationships are still desired, and we know how important being loved is from experience and from reading God's Word.

We will never be able to fully comprehend how much Jesus loves us. The human mind is not big enough to fully grasp the totality and God's love. In Heaven, perhaps we will finally begin to know the extent of that love.

God's redeeming love frees us from guilt and fear. God loves us with justifying love. God's love is demonstrated to us by justifying us and declaring us innocent, by faith through Christ. Christ is treated as if He were the sinner, and the sinner is treated as if they were the righteous one. A divine drama indeed.

1 John 3:1

How great is the love of the Father has lavished on us, that we should be called children of God, and that we are.

Romans 8:38-39

For I am convinced that neither death nor life, neither angels nor demons, neither the present nor the future, nor any powers, neither height nor depth nor anything else in all creation, will be able to separate us from the love of God that is Christ Jesus our Lord.

The cross is God's complete expression of love for us. His love fully undeserving, the cross teaches us that forgiveness takes sacrifice especially on our part toward others. The cross teaches about success. Jesus' death might be considered a failure today. Yet, in John 19:30, as He was dying, Jesus said, "It is finished." You see, He succeeded in his mission to do what the Father sent Him here for. To save a dying world. A world dying from sin.

Although we can say with certainty that God loves to save sinners and even the vilest person can be saved, we must also understand and recognize that God is not obligated to save anyone. Furthermore, we must realize that God is not unrighteous by not saving everyone.

Romans 5:8

But God shows His love for us in that we are all sinners, Christ died for us.

God sees each of us as an individual and collectively. In a personal relationship with Him and/or in a relationship with one another, God desires a relationship with us. With you and I. Us. All of us!

God sees us as His beloved children. He has authority, He leads, teaches; He loves His children, He guides, instructs, and even disciplines each of us as He sees fit when called for. A great father works to provide those characteristics to his children.

No one has the greatest father on earth but in the Heavenly realm, we have a father who loves us in impossible ways. A Father we've never seen and yet look into His eyes with every face we meet. As we are all created in the image of God. God also identifies His children as His own.

Romans 8:14

For as many are led by the Spirit of God, they are the sons of God.

Galatians 3:27-28

The first change from the law to grace regarding a believer's position is all who believe in Christ Jesus become "sons of God."

Paul is indicating in this verse a turn from looking toward Israel as a nation to addressing the Galatian believers. The change from "you are children of God" through faith in Jesus Christ, specifically positions believers in God's direction.

God knows us intimately and loves us abundantly without reservation or hesitation. That is a love worth pursuing and love we can and should return exponentially. It is love we cannot get from any other source for there is no love as great as God's love for us. The greatest love is known to mankind.

WHY LOVE

C ertainly, I've loved some people (mostly my children and my husband when I had one) and others not so much or as much as I should. I loved my family members but should have stopped that much sooner than I did.

It was pointed out to me one day, that I owed several people in my life an apology for loving them "less." I was not sure about that and didn't want to do it. That was like a large bitter, uncomfortable pill to swallow. Though I abhor the thought of apologizing, let alone for being careless with my love, I am making it a daily priority to work on the humbling task of loving others harder.

It's very difficult to admit when you've cheated someone out of anything, but short-changing people out of love seemed particularly difficult. I'm generally good at admitting my mistakes, and apologizing comes easy to me but this task was extremely challenging and honestly seemed a bit ridiculous. That makes it hard for me to keep a straight face while trying to seem sincere.

Initially, it was odd and felt uncomfortably stupid to apologize to people. How much I did or didn't love someone was something only I knew and those I loved less had no idea that they weren't getting a full portion of love from me.

It felt extremely uncomfortable for me to tackle this huge undertaking. Exposing the truth to someone for whom I have "loved less" might injure and possibly devastate the recipient of my confession. How could that be helpful? How does one explain such a deficit if asked the impossible question, "why."

My feeling was that people really don't know the extent of my love for them, so why bring it up at all? I was friendly enough with people and that seemed satisfactory to me. In all honesty, I couldn't be more incorrect in my thinking. I don't have to be in a relationship with someone or agree with someone or even like someone. I don't even have to be near someone, but I am required to love them wholeheartedly and keep them in prayer. That is God's great command.

Romans 13:8. NIV

Let no debt remain outstanding, except the continuing debt to love one another, for whoever loves one another has fulfilled the law.

People are capable of perceiving and are intuitive enough to know how much they are liked or loved by someone. If we are honest with ourselves, we can gain a lot of information from eye contact or lack of eye contact and body language regarding how someone feels about us. It's a language unto its own, void of vocalization.

It has been further explained to me that people know when they are loved less because they sense it and as a result, their feelings are hurt. They don't often express those feelings because they are concerned there could be a chance, they're wrong and wish to avoid a scene or embarrassment. It becomes an avenue of doubt where Satan then begins to go to work with his lies. He uses doubt to curtail being openly honest. No one wants to be vulnerable to that. So, we stay silent and instead allow our insides to rumble uncontrollably.

Whether or not there exists a lack of trust or a disagreement between yourself and others, people are still entitled to a full amount of God-given love.

One way to begin loving people harder is to stop the negative talk that takes place in your heart and mind regarding those you are in a relationship with. We all do it and need to shut it down when it takes place. That allows us to consciously let go and think positively about others. Remind yourself you are a servant of Christ and how should you be showing love to one another.

John 13:34 ESV

A new commandment I give to you, that you love one another: just as I have loved you, you also are to love one another.

We are each loved by God with such incredible love, and we are expected to be giving God's love for us to others. God expects His amazing love to transform us through an incredible love experience reserved exclusively for us. God's love is life changing as in no other possible way.

God wants for each of us not only His incredible life-changing love, mercy, and compassion but He wants love from each of us for Himself. Why are we called to love one another?

John 13:34 NIV

A new commandment I give to you, love one another: as I have loved you, so you must love one another.

We are called to love one another as has loved us as God is love. Whoever lives in love, lives in God, and God in them. This is how love is made complete among us so that we will have confidence and assurance on the day of judgment: In this world, we are like Jesus.

1 John 4:16-17 KJV

And we have known and believed the love that God hath to us. God is love, and he that dwelleth in love dwelleth in God, and God in him. Herein is our love made perfect, that we may have boldness in the day of judgment: because as he is, so are we in this world.

Matthew 22:36-39

"Teacher, which is the great commandment in the Law?" And he said to him, "You shall love the Lord your God with all your heart and with all your soul and with all your mind. This is the great first commandment. And the second is like unto it, thou shall love thy neighbor as thyself.

We can obey Jesus' command to love one another by the grace of God alone. What are some ways we can show love to God?

Ways to Express Love for God.

1. 'Walk in all his ways'
2. 'Keep his commandments'
3. 'Cleave unto him'
4. 'Serve him with all your heart and with all the mind'

We can celebrate the fact that we can be sustained with faith, hope, and love. These are all three key virtues that the Christian religion adheres to. And without "love," faith and hope would almost be useless. Once we truly believe in love (as God has loved us as his children from the beginning of creation), then the effects of faith and hope can be fully realized.

Love is one of the many attributes of God. One important aspect out of many. God tells us He is love and wants us to see love as an essential part of His divine character. God's love is kindness, goodness, steadfastness, and faithfulness.

John 13:35 NIV
By this, everyone will know that you are my disciples, if you love one another.

To be called to God is also to be called into action, as in being summoned. Jesus was not just summoning but was instituting a new law to replace the law of Moses. Being called to love one another is to walk in a new law.

Everyone who calls himself a follower of Christ is also called to walk in love. Jesus' call to us was to love one another as He loved us. Our love should be wholehearted and sacrificial. Walking in love includes loving your enemies, your neighbor, yourself, and anyone else you happen upon who needs Christ's love. (Who doesn't need it.) We need love because we were created in Jesus' likeness and image, the very fabric of our being is love and requires love.

This is huge and confessional for fellow Christians who profess to love Christ. However, we frequently skirt the issue and sometimes rely on our earthly feelings and forego the Word of God. Yes, we can be selfish and self-serving. We are poor sinful beggars before Christ.

The only way I see around this predicament is to daily seek God's Word and help. Rely on the Holy Spirit and remind yourself frequently that God's love and the act of sharing it should be first and foremost. The Holy Spirit dwells in us and longs to teach and grow us closer to God.

The only way we can love as God does is because we receive love from him. Apart from Him, we are unable to love to like Him. We come by His love through God's grace.

Romans 13:10 NIV

Love does not harm a neighbor and, therefore, is the fulfillment of the law.

I have felt sadness and conviction about my serious lack of love for others, along with my acute awareness that my anger, which is an act of rebellion against God, deeply affects the kind of relationship I want with my Lord and Savior along with others. We all need a love relationship with Christ that can heal our broken and sinful selves. We are taught love by God's Holy example through the Holy Spirit.

I am greatly loved and treasured and aware I don't deserve it. It is the truth where my feet are solidly planted. To begin the necessary change in my life I need my anger healed. Anger is simply "pain" behaving badly. Healing is needed to receive all the love God has for us and in return, we then are fully able to love others.

I know that when God is redirecting me through His love and concern, I should stop what I'm doing and pay full attention to Him. If I don't, He will continue His campaign in another way to get my attention. He is not going to let an issue slide. God the Father wants us healed. Our healing helps to bring us into a closer relationship with Christ.

Proverbs 4:23 KJV

Keep thy heart with all diligence; for out of it are the issues of life.

Ezekiel 36:25 NIV

And I will give you a new heart, and a new spirit I will put within you; I will remove the heart of stone from you, your heart of stone and give you a heart of flesh.

Our love relationship with God is a delicate dance we do with Him. It is a sacred Holy dance, reserved for each of us. We are taught God's great love and then can be in the world passing on that love and blessing others with it. We become servants of love. Imagine that scenario and what it looks like. A taste of Heaven now but not yet.

When we are blessed, filled, and energized with God's love, we can do, observe, and understand things that we could not before. We begin the journey walking in God's supernatural love. When we are filled with that love, we can better endure pain, become fearless, resist contention, and are renewed with strength to bless and help others in ways we were not accustomed to or aware of.

John 14:1-4 NIV

"Do not let your hearts be troubled. You believe in God, believe also in me. My Father's house has many rooms; if that were not so, would I have told you that I am going there to prepare a place for you? And if I go and prepare a place for you, I will come back and take you to be with me so that you also may be where I am.

Jesus said the greatest command is to love God and the second greatest is to love people. These are the most important things to God. "LOVE!"

Unfortunately, the thing we love most is ourselves, not others. Loving ourselves does not mean we are to worship ourselves or behave as narcissists. God wants us to go through life without self-hatred, disappointments, or insecurities about ourselves. We are however supposed to remember we are created perfectly in God's image.

I pray that love becomes the center of your world and the reason for you to truly learn to love harder. God has breathed life into each of us and along with life, His amazing love.

Be still for a moment, let that thought sink in, and fully appreciate the gift of unconditional love freely given.

10 Ways to Love

1. Listen without interrupting. (Proverbs 18)
2. Give without sparing. (Proverbs 21:26
3. Answer without arguing. (Proverbs 17:1)
4. Speak without accusing. (James 1:19)
5. Share without pretending. (Ephesians 4:15)
6. Pray without ceasing. (Colossians (1:9)
7. Promise without forgetting. (Proverbs 13:12)
8. Trust without wavering. (Corinthians 13:7)
9. Enjoy without complaint. (Philippians 2:4
10. Forgive without punishment. (Colossians 3:1)

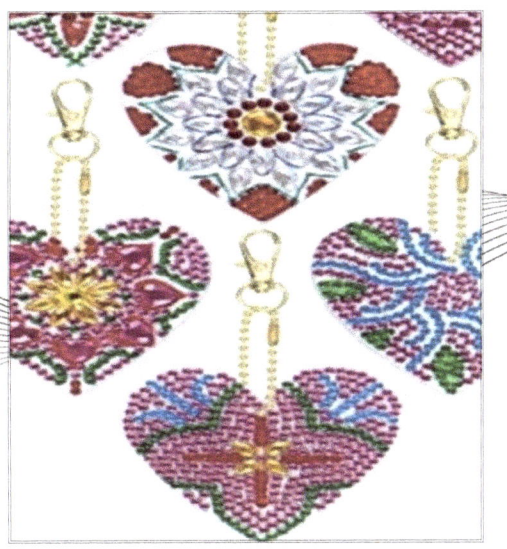

IMPORTANT LOVE

L ove helps us to connect to one another. It also helps us to discover who we are and motivates us into action. Love reforms, refines and teaches us on our journey. It also provides us with a wonderful pleasurable feeling. It is God's way of interacting with us and how He asks us to treat others.

The great command to love one another is the ultimate fulfillment of God's law. When we are obedient to this command we lessen our sin, desire to lie, cheat or even steal from others. With love, our intentions to hurt other people cease. Our love for God becomes motivation to further be obedient to God and His commandments.

God being the creator of all things, created us deliberately and precisely from His love. There is a significant problem of epic proportions that exists as a trap that reveals itself over and over and manages to sabotage and destroy love daily. It is our sinful nature.

This deeper issue is one we all have to wrestle with, "self-centered sin." Another way to put it is, perpetual sin. The sin we love. If we are honest, we do love our sin.

In fact, the majority of conflict is rooted in sin as selfishness. We are wired to view things differently. We insist on having things done our own way and that is sin. In relationships, sin occurs when one or more of us demand to have our own way. When this conflict, division, and strife take place and it is bound to happen, the result is dead or dying love.

God's love is so important because when we are filled with it, we can accomplish, visualize, and understand things that we otherwise could not do or understand, filled with His love.

With God's love, we can endure more pain and suffering, be less fearful, forgive easier, avoid conflict, grow stronger, and be able to bless and attend to others in ways that become a servant of Christ.

2 Corinthians 5:15 MSB

And he died for all, that those who live might no longer live for themselves but only for him who died for them and was raised again.

If you find yourself stuck in a difficult place with your relationships, do something about it. Start with Christ's Word. Don't let anymore time pass while you're missing out on love. Love you need and are entitled to.

This is where God's healing can occur. Don't believe the lies the enemy tells you that whatever mess you're in can't possibly be fixed. That includes the messiness in the world of pain and suffering. We can't but God can and uses us to that end.

Matthew 22:37-39 KJV

Jesus said unto him, Thou shalt love the Lord thy God with all thy heart, and with all thy soul, and with all thy mind.

This is the first and greatest commandment. And the second is like unto it.

Matthew 22:37 KJV

Thou shalt love thy neighbor as thyself.

It seems we are wired to automatically see things "our" way. The problem is our self-centered sin problem. This leads us and often finds us repeating the same mistakes over and over. Sin can become our pleasure and then we are more reluctant to stop the sins we love.

Galatians 6:2 ESV

Bear one another's burdens, and so fulfill the law of Christ.

In college, I had a friend who wore me down emotionally as she was overly dependent and needy. She frequently placed herself wherever I was in the house we shared with twenty-eight others. That it seemed I couldn't escape her was most annoying.

One night in our dinner line she was directly behind me and I was infuriated by that fact. I felt the need to rid myself of her presence by discouraging her and pointing out all the problems and shortcomings she had. I embarrassed and humiliated her. I had truly crossed a line and became mean.

When she began to cry, it made me feel powerful and frightened me at the same time. I had not anticipated her reaction. I thought she might get angry with me, but she collapsed in a heap of tears of sorrow. A sadness I was responsible for. Eventually, she ran to her room.

I was glad she left, but a nagging concern grew in me. I began to think I'd gone too far. My behavior was deplorable and uncalled for. I had wounded her spirit and I thought she might want to harm herself. I went to her room which was locked and could hear her crying on the other side of the door. I couldn't get her to open it up though. I decided to leave her and hope for the best.

A few days later I ran into her, and she seemed fine though she wasn't going to speak to me again. I had earned that response. I wasn't entitled to any attention from her unless it was anger because of my deplorable behavior.

What I did was not love. The pain I inflicted on her could have pushed her over the edge, leaving her wanting to harm herself. That was a horrible and inappropriate thing to do to anyone. It was decidedly disturbing and hateful.

I was not a Christian at the time but that was still no excuse to be so reckless with someone else's heart. I was doing Satan's bidding.

2 Petter 2:1 NIV

But false prophets also arose among the people, just as there will be false teachers among you, who will secretly bring in destructive false teachers among you, who will secretly bring in destructive heresies, even denying the sovereign Lord who bought them, bringing upon themselves swift destruction.

What is so important about love is that love doesn't maim, kill, or annihilate. Love doesn't injure in anyway. Love gives of itself caring and kindness. Love teaches stability and hope. There is safety and security in love. God's love is greater than any other. I am certainly guilty of not loving enough or not loving people harder.

Ephesians 5:1-3 ESV

Therefore, be imitators of God, as beloved children. And walk in love, as Christ loved us and gave himself up for us, a fragrant offering and sacrifice to God. But sexual immorality and all impurity or covetousness must not even be named among you, as is proper among saints.

Romans 6:1-4 ESV

What shall we say then? Are we to continue in sin that grace may abound? By no means! How can we who died to sin still live in it? Do you not know that all of us who have been baptized into Christ Jesus were baptized into his death? We were buried therefore with him by baptism into death, so that, just as Christ was raised from the dead by the glory of the Father, we too might walk in the newness of life.

Why do we allow our sin to damage our love and who we love? We each can behave and move out of the way but prefer for others to accommodate us and move first. We often want what we want, when we want it. This is selfishness unleashed.

It's also easier to love people less whom we don't know well or at all. We often forgo the same accountability with strangers. We can "hit and run" and for the most part get away with bad behavior, especially if it's anonymous. I can be far more impatient and unkinder over the phone where I'm frequently unknown. It is more difficult for me to be unkind or unloving to someone in person.

If there is brokenness in your relationships and you have an opportunity to reconcile, pray harder and try to work on that. Don't let precious time go by, allowing for missed opportunities together, missed memories, and missed love, simply out of stubbornness or pride. It is a tremendous loss.

God wants better for us and has a better plan if we submit and humble ourselves before Him. Where we win and experience God's tremendous love is at the foot of the cross.

There is nothing God can't do or refuses to show up for when a heart needs mending. He longs to provide the way and means to healing. Notice, He can move the most imposing obstacle effortlessly. He is the All-Powerful creator. You are not too big a problem for Him. He has your blueprint and DNA on hand. There is nothing He can't do and does in the name of love.

Jeremiah 1:5 KJV

Before I formed thee in the belly I knew thee, and before thou camest forth out of the womb I sanctified thee, and I ordained thee a prophet unto the nations.

God is intentional with purpose and meaning and always has a plan for our lives. Everything we encounter with God is centered around love. We either love well, love poorly, or a combination of both. Hopefully, we can shift our poor love habits into a purposeful God-centered love fest.

If we are stuck in our pain, sadness, and despair we cannot effectively reach others because we're overly involved in our situation. It's similar to being lost in the woods. It's a special darkness reserved for us by the enemy and liar who wants us lost in sadness and pain.

Acts 26:18 NIV

To open their eyes so they may turn from darkness to light and from the power of Satan to God, that they may rescue forgiveness of sins and a place among those who are sanctified by faith in me.

Colossians 1:12 NIV

He has delivered us from our domain of darkness and transferred us to the kingdom of His beloved Son.

Slowly inhale and exhale. Breathe. We do not have to solely depend on ourselves for change. Our hope lives in Christ.

LOVe IS

W hat is love anyway? Do we need it? Do we want it? Do we recognize it? Are we doing love justice, the way love was intended and deserves? How important is it to truly love one another as we are loved by Christ? Is it bothersome or do you feel justified leaving some people out of your love loop? What is the most important part of love?

Trusting one another completely is one of the most important elements of a relationship. If you are able to trust that your partner won't stray and you trust them with your feelings, that can give you a sense of security in a relationship. You have to trust one another enough in order to be vulnerable on an emotional and physical level.

Loving each other is how we are to live together. It is how we can make a difference and the vehicle by which we live out our God-given faith. It is not random or arbitrary. It's a command. It does often come with obstacles though. We are imperfect sinners with Satan the liar looming in wait for us. He sets attractive traps to catch us in, and our sinful nature obliges.

Pain and suffering from those who should be protecting and loving us muddies the water. This creates confusion and distrust about love and is precisely where Satan wants people trapped. Fearing and distrusting love. We can even question God our Father's love for us as a result of a traumatic past.

When I committed myself to the Lord 43 years ago it took me 30 years to finally trust God. That was a precarious relationship. I desperately needed God but couldn't trust Him. God, however, never left my side despite my doubts, insecurities, and fears.

Eventually, I stopped being angry with God over my difficult and challenging upbringing and grew into the knowledge and wisdom of my past. I began to look upon my horror show upbringing as something that grew me into a smarter, more compassionate, and understanding human. I had been in places I wouldn't wish on my worst enemy and yet I didn't just survive the trauma ordeals, I ultimately thrived. I gained wisdom beyond that of a satisfactory upbringing. That is God's handiwork and promise to work all things for good.

Love is more necessary than money. If love is missing from the equation, it's harder for us to work, and remain physically and emotionally healthy. Love solidifies desire and compatibility with other humans.

When love is valued, we become more willing to sacrifice for and support people through good and bad times. We are willing to be vulnerable to others. When we love others, we respect each other's feelings and boundaries.

If we have been deeply wounded or violated by someone, that may feel like justification for people to exempt themselves from love. Love becomes frightening instead of pleasurable. We will second guess it and have difficulty trusting love. This doesn't have to be a lifelong sentence but with help, fears can be lessened. Trauma responses can be reprogrammed. God longs to free broken hearts so that they can properly love and receive genuine love.

Must we be in a relationship with someone in order to love them unconditionally? We do not have to be friends with everyone or have a relationship with someone to properly love them. Some people may be toxic to us. Are there different degrees of love that are acceptable in God's eyes? There are not. We are to love everyone equally and harder.

Do evil people, such as criminals or murderers get excused from love? Are we loving one another according to the way God's great command directs us? Why or why not? Does love to become more of a substantial challenge knowing what we do about Christ's sacrificial love for us?

Is there ever a reason to withdraw or withhold love from someone? What does God's Word teach us about unconditional love? Is unconditional love acceptance undesirable behavior? No, it never is. We can and need to separate what someone does from who someone is. They aren't the same thing.

Unconditional love is love without strings attached. It's love you offer freely. You simply love someone and want nothing more than their happiness. This type of love is sometimes called compassionate or Agape love.

Agape is "the highest form of love and charity" and "the love of God for man and of man for God". It is in contrast to philia, brotherly love, or philautia which is love of self. Agape love is a profound love that is sacrificial and continues regardless of what circumstances take place. Selfless or sacrificial love is the highest level of love we can offer another. Agape love is a decision to spread love and charity to everyone under all circumstances.

Take a deeper look into the mystery of love from the one true God who brought us life and love. Recognizing God gave us life, we might also be able to learn to love as God intended for us and our lives.

Mark 12:29-30 KJV

And Jesus answered him, the first of all the commandments is, Hear, O Israel; The Lord our God is one Lord: And thou shalt love the Lord thy God with all thy heart, and with all thy soul, and with all thy mind, and with all thy strength: this is the first commandment.

Love releases into our bodies, "feel good" hormones and neurochemicals that trigger specific positive reactions. Love is often more important than money. Self-love (not selfish love) is important because it aids in our ability to love others.

Love feels like security and stability though it is decidedly different for everyone. It is associated with steady amounts of trust. One does not worry about people suddenly leaving you when they're in love.

God could not have been any clearer in His Word. We need to put love into practice, loving people harder.

John 15:12-13 NIV

"My command is this: Love each other as I have loved you. Greater love has no one than this: to lay down one's life for one another.

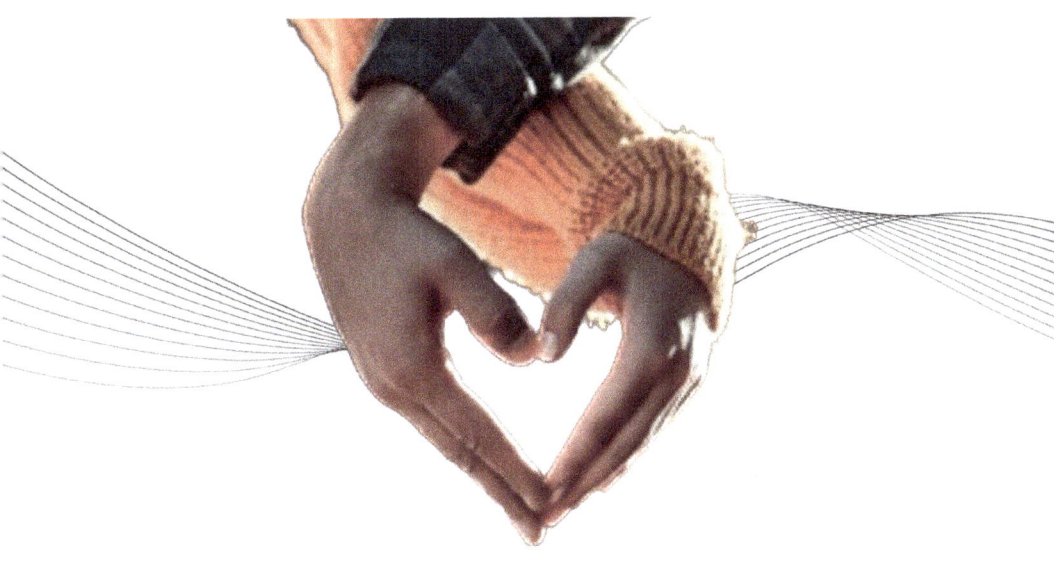

WHAT LOVE

1 Corinthians 13:4-8 ESV

Love is patient and kind; love does not envy or boast; it is not arrogant or rude. It does not insist on its own way; it is not irritable or resentful; it does not rejoice at wrongdoing but rejoices with the truth.

Love is friendship that has caught on fire. Love, for me and many is hard! It can be tricky to navigate. As individuals we all have a different love language and currency that fits our individual love needs. It can be so overwhelming as to cause some to refrain from love relationships altogether. Especially challenging are intimate relationships with a partner. Other love relationships may ebb and flow. All relationships, especially love relationships require attention and maintenance and conscious work.

I'm extremely resilient. I have emotional setbacks but get going again when I need to. It's important for me to have resolution and understanding about my feelings and my relationships. It is how I learn and grow. It is also my way of achieving closure and does not require participation by anyone else. It's taking personal inventory of a relationship and understanding how it worked or didn't work.

Sometimes love leaves us in unpredictable ways. Our spouse may find some other love interest or just desire to be free from the responsibilities of the relationship. Friends we've known and loved for many years may just decide to turn away without provocation or explanation. Oftentimes children might decide to choose estrangement from their parents without notice or discussion.

There are also individuals who suffer from rejection sensitive dysphoria (RSD). It's an extreme emotional sensitivity and resulting pain triggered by the perception that they have been rejected or criticized by important people in their life. It may also be triggered by a sense of not meeting their own high standards or others' expectations. People who have RSD don't handle rejection well. For example, when friends don't respond to a text message right away, answer a phone call or return your call, a rejection-sensitive individual might think, "They no longer want to be friends with me." Someone without rejection sensitivity might be more likely to assume that their friend is just too busy to reply.

Rejection sensitivity can cause numerous issues in personal and romantic relationships, and lead to problems like depression and anxiety. Being overly sensitive to judgment, criticism, and rejection can lead to frequent misunderstandings and unhealthy relationships.

People can also have an avoidant personality disorder. They are very sensitive to anything critical, disapproving, or mocking because they constantly think about being criticized or rejected by others. They are hyper-vigilant for any sign of rejection.

Rejection is a very real physical pain in the brain. When rejection-sensitive dysphoria is activated, the individual experiencing it must be able to vocalize how they're feeling. This helps lessen the painful symptoms associated with being rejected.

Sometimes individuals are overly sensitive to criticism which can be a result of having a high emotional IQ. This means they are empathetic and have an awareness of their impact on others. However, if the criticism is becoming too much and it's affecting your mental health and sense of self-worth, it's important to understand when to take a step back.

The most telling marker of rejection-sensitive dysphoria is an extreme response to real or imagined rejection that one believes is taking place. Most people will probably feel some sadness, disappointment, or frustration after experiencing rejection. But for those with RSD, rejection or criticism can be overwhelming enough to lead to outbursts of rage, panic, and intense sadness.

People with RSD feel "excessive" pain, usually in their limbs or extremities. They may also experience changes in body temperature, unusual sweating, a decreased range of motion, shortness of breath, chest pains, and other symptoms.

If you are suddenly abandoned by someone, you can wait for your friend to return but they aren't likely to come back. Most likely you will never have an answer for how or why a relationship ended. Help yourself to move on from other people's behavior. It's not about you, it's about them.

Sometimes adult children walk away from their parents and become silent. It's important to acknowledge the child you raised and sacrificed for has turned away. Adult children don't just walk away from traumatic childhoods, they leave parents who worked very hard to be good parents too.

No parent is perfect, but some parents choose harm and trauma when raising a family. Others try to avoid the same pitfalls they experienced in their childhood but can miss the mark and trauma occurs anyway. Trauma can bleed into relationships and families for generations.

Many parents work overtime and sacrifice themselves for their children. They view their parenting responsibilities as a mission field and give all they have to their children. Committed and thoughtful child rearing happens with awareness, planning, and when one desires to change a person's own childhood experience.

Continue to love and pray for your children as adults, even if you are estranged from them. Grieve the loss. Acknowledge your anger as pain. Seek support and learn ways to move on and appreciate your ongoing friendships. Get involved in life. God still has a plan for you. You are more than just a parent. You are God's child.

In love relationships, the level of commitment sometimes changes. Not spending enough time together or complicated emotions might arise such as anger or jealousy. If not given enough attention, these issues can end relationships. But people don't fall out of love. Love is a choice.

Psalm 136:26 NIV

Give thanks to the God of Heaven, for His love endures forever.

Romans 5:8 NIV

But God demonstrated his own love for us in this. While we were still sinners, Christ died for us.

God's love is perfect and can be believed and trusted. It is where our freedom and security lies. It is how we develop the necessary love skills required in each of us to then lovingly serve others as we are commanded to do.

In the world today love of money has become more important than anything else. We work to provide for ourselves and our families, but without love, there is little left to be inspirational or provide that get-up-and-go attitude for us to work harder.

When we choose to love others harder, we become encouraged and our sense of purpose and desire to do well and succeed occurs. This leaves us with a substantial feeling of security and fullness. We have more of ourselves to give to those we care about and love.

1 Corinthians 15:58 ESV

"Whatever work you do, do it with all your heart. Do it for the Lord and not for men. Remember that you will get your reward from the Lord.

Proverbs 17:17 NIV

A friend loves at all times, and a brother is born in a time of adversity.

In all things love harder, at play, at leisure, and at work. Even in your disappointment and sadness choose to love everyone harder.

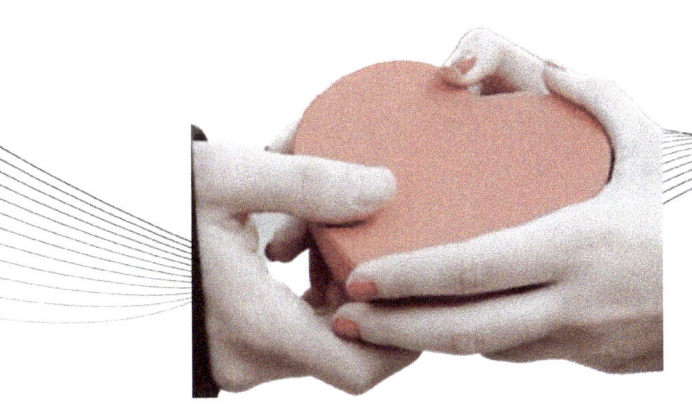

scary Love

Philophobia is the extreme fear of falling in love or developing an emotional connection. There is additional fear in attaining that connection with someone.

Most people consider love a "happy" thing. While this is a satisfying narrative, there are many who suffer from loneliness, desire and attachment disorders. Love can often be challenging. Not because you might not have a love relationship but because it really can be frightening to some people.

New relationships are considered uncharted territory, and many people have natural fears of the unknown. Letting oneself fall in love means taking a giant leap of faith. You are placing a great amount of trust in another person whom you don't know, allowing them to affect you, which makes one feel exposed and vulnerable.

Falling in love can be exciting and thrilling, but for many people, it can be extremely frightening. The thought of having to trust someone with your emotions is not as easy as it might seem. Imagine what might happen if my heart is broken or my emotions betrayed?

Many negative thoughts can stem from people's past, including their childhoods, leaving them feeling especially vulnerable and afraid to take a risk.

One might test people in their relationships subconsciously. This can actually lead to misunderstandings and sabotaging a relationship instead of nurturing it.

It has been hard for me to believe or trust in love. Trauma from the past can have that effect on its victims. Love isn't always perfect because we are not sinners. The only perfect love is the love of Christ. Perfect love from Christ is bestowed upon us, undeservingly. When we find ourselves in love, it can be a genuine struggle, blessing or both. God's love is the only love that is pure and perfect.

God's love is also steadfast and unchanging. It springs from His infinite goodness and mercy. Jesus demonstrated that love by blessing and serving the poor, the sick and those in distress. There is no greater love than that of Christ's perfect love. We are loved and by that love are able to bestow love to others. We should learn to receive with gratitude, God's amazing one of a kind love.

Love can stir up fears and insecurities for many people. It seems the more love you have, the more love you stand a chance of losing. Falling in love requires one to recognize powerful feelings of longing, which can leave a person emotionally exposed. The more a person means to us the more afraid we can become of losing that person. Allow yourself to be vulnerable and fall in love.

Our fears are not only just that we can lose someone we love but we can also become aware of our own fragile human state. More reasons why we need God in our lives and relationships. We cannot ever lose or be rejected by Him.

My closest and dearest friend has loved me for fifty seven years. I love her right back. My closest friend in my hometown has loved me for nearly forty years. My church family loves me as a sister in Christ. I have many more friends who love me and God loves me deeply. I'm an abundantly loved child of God.

How to identify real love:

*Real love makes us feel vulnerable.
*New love stirs up past wounds.
*Love challenges old identities.
*With real joy comes real pain.
*Love can often be unequal.
*Relationships can break family connections.
*Love can stir up existing fears.

Most of the relationships we enter into supply us with an onslaught of emotions and challenges. Understanding how fear of intimacy forms behaviors is an important key to having a satisfactory and fulfilling relationship. We often allow our fears to take over when things aren't working out and are surprised to learn we may be sabotaging our relationships.

We need to develop workable solutions and ways to cope with deeper concerns and challenges in relationships. God's Word is full of truth and wisdom to carry into a relationship, in order to increase the likelihood, it succeeds.

We are a family of sinners. We get angry and upset with each other and often choose to love some people less or not at all. That is not acceptable in God's eyes. We owe those people in our lives, whom we have not fully loved according to God's great command, an apology. Loving someone less requires a genuine correction of conscience and a heartfelt apology.

While I did not have supportive love from my biological family, I was shown love from others outside of my family. God generously put people in my journey to be loved. Those love interventions taught me love I hadn't known before. It provided a foundation of love that helped me to love my own children and be a better mother.

I love others. It isn't hard to love my children and extended family. It can be difficult to love people who have wronged me in some manner. I also love my church family. Love does not require a relationship. You can love and pray for people in your life but disconnect from them physically and emotionally if they are difficult or toxic. You can love people who are far away from you as readily as those who are physically close. People who you need distance from can become your daily prayer projects.

Sometimes in our differences and conflicts our love turns to anger. This diminishes our love capacity, and we are then in sin, leaving us outside the will of God.

Our personal feelings really don't matter in the face of God's commands. We are to be faithful and obedient to God's Word not to our personal desires and issues.

Love, even unconditional love does not mean unconditional acceptance of everything someone does. God loves His children unconditionally yet chastises and disciplines us when necessary. God clearly identifies sin in His Word.

The most common reason it's so hard to fall in love is fear of commitment. That can be terrifying to some people. Uncertainty about where the relationship stands is also a scary prospect. Fear that if you commit to the relationship, the relationship might fail, and you are avoiding pain and loss. There can be a lingering fear of being a victim of abuse in a relationship. Especially if abuse and trauma are in your past.

It is a worthy cause to be sober and mindful in all relationships. If the relationship does develop, love yourself right into it or out of it.

Do not accept or contend with abuse and deceit. One can offer the argument that Jesus Himself turned the other cheek. He did not, however, walk into the slap. None of us are called into victim roles.

We must remember to become resilient and resolved to God's love for us even in our pain. You have never been abandoned or forsaken by God even in your darkest moments.

John 4:18 ESV

There is no fear in love. But perfect love casts out fear, because fear has to do with punishment. The one who fears has not been perfected in love.

Deuteronomy 31:6 NIV

Be strong and courageous. Do not be afraid or terrified because of them, for the LORD your God goes with you; he will never leave you nor forsake you."

Love Language

G od created a very specific love language for us. He wants us to know and feel the intense love He has for all that He has created. There are five love languages that live on a spectrum. It is possible to learn to speak all five them.

If you can learn and understand your partner's love language, it can help you discern how your partner shows their love. This will help you to feel loved and appreciated. In turn we can learn the ways in which a partner gives their love differently than how you share yours.

There are five love languages:

1. Words of admiration.
2. Acts of service.
3. Gifts.
4. Quality time.
5. Physical touch.

The strongest of these love languages is "quality" time. Quality time is just as important spent with God our father. We do that by making God a priority and by being intentional with our time. Setting aside distractions and often times listening to the Bible on audio can be a great choice especially in a car.

In our personal relationships, knowing or learning others love language and them knowing yours is helpful to feel loved and appreciated. It is one of the simplest ways to improve your relationships.

Luke 19:10 NIV

For the Son of man came to seek and to save the lost.

2 Peter 3:9 NIV

The Lord is not slow in keeping his promise, as some understand slowness. Instead, he is patient with you, not wanting anyone to perish, but everyone to come to repentance.

Love is a noun and a verb. It's the opposite of hatred. Like and love are not the same and may not be applicable together. Love is a set of emotions and behaviors characterized by intimacy, passion, and commitment. It involves care, closeness, protectiveness, attraction, affection, and trust. Love can vary in intensity and can change over time. It is possible to love from afar.

To say one does not love and is not loved describes a person completely emotionally void, detached and isolated from the love of others.

Some people are cautious and slow to accept love but do not reject sincere love. It may take time to trust in love and one may test it but can and do most often accept it. We are also quite capable of taking love for granted.

Love may be difficult and challenging if one has an abusive or traumatic history but it's possible to understand what love is and should look like. I'm certain many have difficulties with love which is why they seek understanding of it and themselves. They are not without love but may seem illusive.

What many often lack are specific skills to help them accomplish their personal goals pertaining to difficult love relationships. Trauma interferes and often confounds that process at times.

That does not make these particular individuals loveless, that makes them damaged. Damage can be repaired the not entirely eliminated. One can live successfully in the aftermath of trauma and abuse. All is not lost in Christ.

Love never fails and always wins in the end.

1 Corinthians 13:8 NIV

Love never fails. But where there are prophecies, they will cease where there are tongues, they will be stilled; where there is knowledge, it will pass away.

Are you trying to get God to come to you and show up how you need Him to be, or are you running to Him in order to know Him on His terms?

Each one of us is deeply and unconditionally loved by God. That too for me was difficult love to accept, but through understanding God's Word, I've grown into acceptance of God's love and the promises attached to it.

There seems to be a difference between the words "love" and "loves." The difference happens in the use of "we" and "they." As previously stated love is both a noun and a verb. Love is used in subjects such as he, she, and they. Loves is used after plural subjects like he and she.

Don't wait to be intellectually stimulated by God's Word but be prepared to have your heart beat with His and have your soul on fire for His companionship and company. Be transformed, not just informed. Feel God's passion and pass on that knowledge, hunger and thirst to your neighbor.

Loving harder can come from being loved hard in return. God loves you harder than anyone.

The word love in itself and without any context is generally a noun. The difference occurs when an "S" is added to the end of the word love it becomes a verb.

When love is active it becomes a verb.

- Love is a friendship that has caught fire.
- Love is composed of a single soul inhabiting two bodies.
- Love is the only force capable of transforming an enemy into a friend.
- Since love grows with you, so beauty grows.

We are broken. We're often uncertain. We question and test. As much as we love ourselves, we are still capable of love and can be loved in return.

What actually keeps our relationships strong, year after year if none of us has love for each other? We don't just tolerate and humor each other but we love and demonstrate that love to one another to the best of our abilities. We love according to the past modeling we've witnessed and by receiving Christ's unfailing love.

THE LOOK OF LOVE

Throughout our lives we are compiling a picture of what love looks like to us. This process begins early and eventually we imagine a soulmate and perfect person to spend our life with. However, the reality of love does not often match the fantasy version of love we conjured in our hearts and minds.

By carefully observing people it's possible to discover the sources of their individual happiness and joy. Using discernment, one can also evaluate what money can afford people. We know that money can make oneself feel secure and comfortable. Secure finances allows one freedom, relief and personal pleasure. It also offers additional opportunities to achieve specific goals.

Money, however, cannot buy anyone respect, love, trust, or creative abilities. Money isn't love. It can create a certain happiness that can lend itself to love but unless your plans are to rain money on people you love, so they feel loved, money is just money.

A true loving relationship should reflect affection, trust, respect and appreciation along with ongoing open and honest communication. If these attributes are in place one can consider the relationship as healthy and comprised of true love.

Love involves feelings of affection, attachment, desire and need. These feelings can be sudden or build over time including attraction and respect. Love can also include fleeting emotions of care, concern and commitment along with respecting and helping one another.

Most of us long for something or someone to love. All of us need love to be emotionally and physically healthy. It is said that physical contact with others, hugs, handshakes and touching are daily requirements for emotional health. I try to make physical contact with others as often as I can.

I once encountered a homeless man while having lunch with my aunt at a restaurant. He came in and sat quietly. My aunt and I bought him a meal of his choosing. I rubbed his back during my conversation with him. I couldn't imagine being homeless and not having human contact because of being unkempt and unclean. He was entitled to human touch as well as a meal.

Love and physical contact aids and strengthens our cardiovascular system keeping it in good shape.

John 15:9 NLT

"As the Father loved me, I too have loved you. Remain in my love."

The Good News: Jesus loves us, just as God the Father loved him. In this truth we can rest secure and at peace.

Love requires far less energy to sustain than anger. Our body reacts and assumes the brunt of our brains emotions. Our strong emotions, especially negative ones affect our cell structures and most importantly our immune system. This leaves us more susceptible to infections and poor health. That results in a difficult and challenging life of ongoing problems.

Letting go of anger and understanding that anger is pain, (pain behaving badly) is a process by which you can reduce the chances of becoming a professional patient, always coping with a new ailment or treatment.

Fortunately for us, we are always being loved. God loved us before we were ever formed. We are drenched in His love. God longs to be our contentment, we have a happy place, a safe harbor in Jesus.

Jeremiah 1:5 KJB

"Before I formed you in the womb I knew you;

Before you were born I sanctified you; I ordained you a prophet to the nations."

God created man with the ability to love as He is love incarnate. Love is a combination of who God is, what God can do, and what He has done. God's response to everything is always love.

1 John 4:8 NIV

Whoever does not love does not know God, because God is love.

As a general rule, love mostly requires an object, compassion, and commitment. However, we can love an idea, concept, feeling, place, or even plans we make. Though the Bible describes love as personal between persons, there are definitely far more applications for love.

Love as a verb is best observed and understood through actions. You know you are loved by how you are treated, more so than professions of love. Love is selfless and wants the best for everyone. It has and demonstrates genuine concern for one another and all humanity.

As we are created in the image of God, we are also created with the idea planted in our hearts about the importance and desire for love. Our greatest love should always be God, next in line is our neighbor.

All religions recognize love. Christian theology recognizes the importance of love in the forefront because God has revealed that He is love by sending His only Son to die on the cross in order to save us from our sins. When we love someone else it is the recognition of the essence of God's Devine presence in another person.

Every civilization, community or social group, even civilizations completely separated from others has worshiped something. That is because it is built into our nature to worship. That worship properly realized, should be to God the Father.

As we are each created in God's image, I try to look into the faces of others and remind myself I'm getting a glimpse of God Himself when speaking to them.

Being loved should encompass compassion, dedication, and loyalty. This is how we are loved by God completely, unconditionally, and with purpose. Unconditional love does not include unconditional acceptance. You can love someone and still be in disagreement with them and there be consequences for inappropriate behavior.

We often seek to understand what the purpose of love is. Love is the desire and willingness to be actionable in love. To be there for someone else including to support them and help them grow; to make a difference in someone's life; to share in and care about someone else's happiness and struggles other than our own. We are to be demonstrative about our love, even when it's hard. Especially when you don't really want to.

When you are fully loved it's like being secure in your home, or finding and feeling secure in your true self and realizing that you are not alone. In reality, we are never alone as God is ever present (omnipresent) and will never leave us. There is security in this promise as God does not lie. We can be assured that everything in God's Word is the truth.

Romans 11:1-2 NIV

I ask then: Did God reject his people? By no means! I am an Israelite myself, a descendant of Abraham, from the tribe of Benjamin.

Romans 5:8 NIV

But God demonstrates his love for us in this: While we were still sinners, Christ died for us.

Christians are to be known by the fact that they love God and others. Their love is not necessarily as the world views it and is visible by how we speak along with behavior and actions. It is identifiable by what Christians do, not just by what they say. Staying aware that we are representing an entire group of God-fearing believers by our actions should help us to behave. This has an ongoing learning curve. We are after all sinful by nature. We also love our sins more than we confess.

Luke 6:32-36 NKJV

"But if you love those who love you, what credit is that to you? For even sinners love those who love them. And if you do good to those who do good to you, what credit is that to you? For even sinners do the same. And if you lend to those from whom you hope to receive back, what credit is that to you? For even sinners lend to sinners to receive as much back. But love your enemies, do good, and lend, hoping for nothing in return; and your reward will be great, and you will be sons of the Highest. For He is kind to the unthankful and evil. Therefore, be merciful, just as your Father also is merciful.

We are often being watched and judged by non-Christians along with our Christian family. It's important not just because we might be watched but because we should be on our best behavior at all times. Our attitudes, our love, and the way we act are meant to be a reflection of God's love. Jesus said that only two commands are needed as a demonstration of our faith in Christ in our daily lives. It is love of God and love of neighbor. All of the laws and prophecies are fulfilled in such love.

In Love

A t any given time, most of us will have the opportunity to experience the feeling of love outside the bounds of familial love. Your heart may flutter when you see or think of your love interest. Spending time with your one special person can bring on genuine euphoria.

Being in love is a part of life that many people long to experience. Love is seen around us in our world daily on television, in books and by observing folks walking down the street together hand in hand.

Being in love feels wonderful and our body responds by releasing hormones that set in motion very specific positive reactions. Love increases our levels of dopamine which keeps us hooked on love. It becomes like an addiction and when suddenly taken from us, we experience real genuine pain. Both emotional and physical.

When our minds react to love it also affects our bodies. It is not surprising that we are seeking out love, as a way to feel better physically.

I fell in love my freshman year at college. It was a tumultuous, emotionally and physically dangerous relationship but my brain kept telling me I was deeply in love and could not exist without that particular person. I didn't actually receive much love from my partner or the other residents in the house we lived in. That relationship was an extremely flimsy interpretation of what love was, yet I was hooked.

When the relationship ended because of cheating on his part, I felt like I would die. I couldn't sleep or eat. I cried, screamed and paced endlessly. That lasted week, before it began to subside. My anxiety was unbearable and uncontrollable. Love was gone and I felt abandoned and lost.

A physical relationship is not in and of itself love. There are confines dictated to us in Scripture about the acceptable conditions for sex. The only place it is sanctioned is in marriages. Anything outside of that is sin.

Sadly, I have been involved in sinful relationships in my younger years and felt convicted about them and sought confession with my priest once. Expecting forgiveness, I was shocked by his statement "if it feels good, it can't be bad." That was the only comment I received. I left dismayed and unsatisfied with that unholy and unbiblical response. I knew that was not a satisfactory answer.

Eventually I ended that relationship and left the church where affairs were rampant including with the priest himself. It was an openly sinful church, lacking moral fortitude. That is where I learned the phrase" in love with our sin."

A physical relationship outside of marriage is an unacceptable love relationship. Surely designed to separate you from God. Satan will use feelings of pleasure and call them love in order to snare you into his trap.

Knowing God's Word and feeling well grounded in its understanding helps one avoid the sins of the flesh. Man's response is to seek love and pleasure above a relationship with God in many instances.

1 John 4:8 KJV

And we have known and believed the love that God hath to us. God is love; and he that dwelleth in love dwelleth in God, and God in him.

Love doesn't purposefully do anything wrong to a neighbor or friend. Anything negative is not love though it may be mistaken or attributed to love. God's greatest command is to love Him and one another, at all times.

When we are passionately dedicated and consistent, love is reinforced, and a sense of security develops when we love others.

When evaluating personal happiness, it's important to understand the value of a situation and reflect on it soberly and wisely. There is a direct correlation proportionate to the amount of love we have in our lives, as a reflection of love received, and love given.

Mark 12:31 ERV

"The second most important command is this: Love your neighbor the same as you love yourself. These two commands are the most important.

Romans 13:8-10 NKJV

Owe no one anything except to love one another, for he who loves another has fulfilled the law. For the commandments, "You shall not commit adultery," "You shall not murder," "You shall not steal," "You shall not bear false witness," "You shall not covet," and if there is any other commandment, are all summed up in this saying, namely, "You shall love your neighbor as yourself." Love does not harm a neighbor; therefore, love is the fulfillment of the law.

LOVE INTERRUPTED

N one of us will get out of here alive! We don't have an unlimited amount of time on earth. All of us will die. Making the best we can out of whatever circumstances we are dealing with takes hope and courage. People are not always predictable or happy. They have baggage proportionate to their circumstances.

Have you ever had the feeling that sometimes your partner has emotionally shut down? That a communication gap exists between you and is growing exponentially by the day? This can often be the case when one partner can't relate with themself or the relationship any longer. It's easy to get stuck thinking and believing that the significant love bond between you has run dry. Does that really mean the relationship is over?

Recognizing a chasm forming does not have to spell the end. This is where loving harder comes into play and keeping God in the forefront is essential.

If you've ever witnessed a horrendous accident or some tragic event that you think only happens to other people, think again. They happen every day. In fact, a motor vehicle accident occurs every 60 seconds.

When I was a young teenager, I happened to be driving on a four-lane road in our town. I had just recently acquired my first driver's license. I was driving in the inside lane and a semi-truck was neck and neck with me in the far-right lane. Out of nowhere, having crossed two lanes of traffic on the opposite side of the road, going in the opposite direction a small boy approximately 8 years old darted in front of my car. Fortunately, I was able to stop in time narrowly avoiding hitting him. Passing my vehicle, he landed in front of the semi-truck which was not as capable of stopping abruptly. The semi-driver struck the boy. The driver of the truck was incapable of stopping his rig in time.

It was the most gruesome thing I'd ever witnessed. The truck driver pulled over to the shoulder. He then exited the cab of the truck and went over to the shoulder, laid his head on the ground, and sobbed uncontrollably. The boy's mother who witnessed the event ran into the street and was screaming over her dead child's body for someone to help him. That was impossible. The boy's head exploded and shot as far as ten feet across the road. It was the most horrific sight I've ever witnessed. There was no help possible that could bring the boy back.

I could not speak and could barely breathe. Cars were passing by, and people were going on their way. I was so confused. Why hadn't the world stopped? A boy was dead. Didn't the earth realize the horror that had occurred? Why were people continuing their day as if everything were normal?

I always thought that accidents or horrendous events were things that happened to other people and that my life and my loved ones were immune to tragedies such as that. While it wasn't one of my family members, it happened right in front of me. How naive I was. Random tragic acts happen around us all the time. I witnessed someone's loved one die in front of me. It is forever etched in my brain. It travels with me everywhere. I will always remember it.

Armed with this gruesome sight and new knowledge of death, I am reminded to love everyone in my life harder still. Relatives, friends and strangers. Tomorrow may never come for any of us. Life is fragile and a gift we should hold onto with tenderness and care.

Romans 6:23 NIV

For the wages of sin are death but the gift of God is eternal life in Christ Jesus our Lord.

Ephesians 2:8 NASB-1995

For it is by grace you have been saved through faith; and that not of yourselves, it is the gift of God.

Revelations 22:17 NASB

The Spirit and the bride say, "Come." And let the one who hears say, "Come." And let the thirsty one come; let the one who desires, take the water of life without cost.

We cannot change tragic events in our lives or do anything about mistakes in the past, but we can choose to live today in such a way that tomorrow can be more positive and healing. Allows us additional serenity and hope. It's a choice to change and grow. Hard emotional work pays off, in the form of added peace, hope, and stability. All gifts from our Lord.

We prayed for the boy who died and the hurting broken family of the boy. We did not leave out the truck driver. So many possibilities of what and how things went wrong but surely the short answer is sin. We honor and bless those who mourn. That accident required a gentle and heartfelt harder love response. The friend with me and I genuinely and sincerely grieved that loss. It was a shock to our system. We were young teenagers. It was a traumatic and horrific loss of life to witness.

ALWAYS CHOOSE LOVE

C hoose to love as Christ commands. Fight hard against cutting people off emotionally and refuse to initiate it. Put aside meaningless pettiness with the people you love.

A few of my family members allowed their differences with my mother to keep them distant for long periods despite her efforts to reconcile. Today, after she is no longer with us, their regret is profound. Don't make the same mistakes in your life.

Even if you feel that you've been wronged, always choose to forgive and seek reconciliation. If reconciliation isn't possible, pray harder and turn the matter over to God.

Forgiveness is a gift you give yourself that flows from God. Holding a grudge takes an enormous emotional, spiritual, and psychological toll on people. Letting go, on the other hand, frees you from the shackles of the past.

To get started, pray and enter into God's realm through His Word. You will soon get to know Him on the wonderful and miraculous journey you are embarking on. Learning and living a true and pure relationship based on love. You will get to know God's undeniable, unrelenting love along the way.

God provides the exact blueprint for our journey in the Bible. There is nothing we can do to become a better person on our own. We need God to grow into better people.

It is also important to understand the differences between the law and the Gospel. Knowing the theological distinction is important to understand. Distinguishing between law and the Gospel has genuine implications for daily living. It also impacts our spiritual life.

The law is what condemns us but Christ through His death on the cross became our only salvation and way to the Father. The law is command given by God for humanity.

The Gospel is what the law can't do and that is to offer forgiveness and dignity to those with guilt and shame.

We are not capable of obeying God's law perfectly. That is why God sent His only Son to save and free us from ourselves. Christ restores our relationship and fellowship with God the Father.

Galatians 3:13 NIV

Christ redeemed us from the curse of the law by becoming a curse for us, for it is written: "Cursed is everyone who is hung on a pole."

The law teaches us:

Galatians 3:24 KJV

Wherefore the law was our schoolmaster to bring us unto Christ, that we might be justified by faith.

The new law (the law of Christ) the new commandment is to "love one another."

Being saved by grace alone is not the law.

1 John 4:20 KJV

"If a man says, I love God, and hateth his brother, he is a liar: for he that loveth not his brother whom he hath seen, how can he love God whom he hath not seen?"

God offers each of us a wonderful plan for our lives. God loves us so dearly He wants us for eternity. In His perfect love, He sent us His only son so that we might learn to know Him more intimately.

We were each specifically created from God's great love for us. His wish is to spend all of eternity with the people He created. He longs for us to know, desire and enjoy a personal relationship with Him.

When choosing love, it generally means treating others kindly. Through acts of love and kindness, close attention and understanding of other people and standing up for the rights of others we begin to achieve some of God's intentions for us. With ongoing acts of love, God's light shines for those in need. We always have opportunities to love harder.

PURPOSEFUL LOVE

W hy love on purpose? Acting with intention is an action that requires purpose, and a voice. When being purposeful about love, it's important to ensure that you are soberly and intentionally giving yourself unconditionally along with acceptance and forgiveness to others. Count yourself a complete person before entering into a relationship with someone else. This means you are not dependent on having a particular person's love in order to carry on in life. God's love is sufficient and sacrificial.

We must not try and assume our identity from those who love us or by being in a love relationship with a partner. Our identity can be found only in Christ as we are His beloved.

A purposeful relationship is one where all parties can benefit from knowing each other. Not a relationship that requires equal reciprocation back and forth, but an honest give-and-take relationship. Love shouldn't keep score.

Ways to be purposefully in love are through words that uplift, receiving and giving gifts, being of service, physical touch, and the all-important quality time spent with those whom we love. We must prayerfully pursue these endeavors to receive what God intends for us through them. If it seems as if love is too much work, keep in mind, we inherited God's "love" gene, metaphorically speaking. We were born and wired for the job. If we always enter into the love arena with prayer, seeking Him first in our hearts, God longs to be our ever-present help.

Acts 20:35 NIV

In everything I did, I showed you that by this kind of hard work, we must help the weak, remembering the words the Lord Jesus himself said: 'It is more blessed to give than to receive."

Unfortunately, sin keeps us separated from God and fully knowing and experiencing Him. We do have awareness of our sin and how it separates us which often creates a growing distance in our relationship with Him.

The reality of God's presence does not always stop us from sinning. We do know when we are stuck in perpetual sin. Things such as smoking, having an affair, cheating, stealing, and disobeying rules and laws. Many more examples of perpetual sin exist to trap us.

Love is not always consciously and/or intentionally operating. Sometimes love sneaks up on us. Other times we decide to love someone. It's important to understand our motives or drive. Ask yourself if you're forcing a romantic partnership with someone simply because you think you should or if genuine love and respect taking place.

Isaiah 53:6 NIV

All we like sheep have gone astray; we have turned everyone to our way; the Lord has laid on him the iniquity of us all.

What are the stumbling blocks to love? "Stumbling blocks" is a metaphor for things that get in our way and impede our ability to love as we are called to by Christ. The enemy (Satan) put many stumbling blocks in our path.

Romans 14:13 BSB

Therefore let us not judge one another anymore, but rather decide not to put any stumbling block or obstacle in a brother's way.

Isaiah 57:14 NIV

And it will be said, "Build up, build up, prepare the way. Remove every obstacle out of the way of My people."

1 Corinthians 1:23 NIV

But we preach Christ crucified, to Jews a stumbling block and to Gentiles foolishness,

Revelation 2:14 NASB-1995

But I have a few things against you because you have there some who hold the teaching of Balaam, who kept teaching Balak to put a stumbling block before the sons of Israel, to eat things sacrificed to idols, and to commit acts of immorality.

Love Trauma

When children are traumatized, they look for ways to soothe themselves and this then becomes the foundation for how individuals end up in addiction. Unfortunately, victims have difficulty learning how to express their emotions appropriately because it was never safe to express an emotion without fear of rejection and/or abandonment.

Victims flounder through life in fear of rejection for expressing their true feelings, especially anger. As a result, they often become passive aggressive instead of learning to properly express their emotions and anger with words. Oftentimes the anger becomes outbursts of rage, which is also an inappropriate response.

I have a sister who frequently rages. She became so out of control once that she hit an employee. She didn't even lose her job. She had to attend anger management, but it had no effect on her behavior. I eventually had to extricate myself from my relationship with her because I simply could no longer accept the abuse and angry outbursts. Her behavior was unpredictable and emotionally exhausting to witness.

Victims can stay stuck in this cycle of anger and rage for a lifetime without intervention and tools to cope and help them discover their voice. Victims frequently have intense love for those who have injured them. This is how trauma bonding occurs.

Trauma bonding is when emotional bonds with an individual that arise from a recurring cyclical pattern of abuse happens. This behavior is perpetuated by intermittent reinforcement through rewards and punishments. That is not love. That is emotional destruction.

The process of forming a trauma bond is also referred to as traumatic bonding. It is directly related to and caused by traumatic abuse, whether physical, emotional or verbal. Attachment forms out of growing familiarity with the victim role. It becomes like a second skin. It is almost visible to others though they might not be able to fully understand it.

Love goes a long way to heal these damaged and fragile hearts. It's crucial to show love by listening to them. Listening without comment or advice is the most beneficial and unselfish gift one can give to another. Additionally, pray for and love them daily and harder.

Listening without comment or advice is hard to do. Commenting is similar to an involuntary response like blinking or swallowing. We want to jump in and say something. We do it because it calms us down. This form of fixing and rescuing is not about fixing the victim but it's about fixing oneself. It's an attempt to fix your own uncomfortable feelings with other people's feelings.

An emotional response to a terrible event like an accident, rape or natural disaster, can immediately result in shock and denial which are fairly typical responses. Reactions that linger for longer times include unpredictable emotions, flashbacks, strained relationships and even physical symptoms like headaches or nausea. These are predictable responses to traumatic relationships. We are doomed in our past without God in our present.

Much love and care are required for these victims. Demands or ultimatums do further damage. "Getting over it," isn't a sane or rational possibility. It just becomes guilt tripping and shaming.

Interventions that keep trauma in mind and lovingly guide victims with listening and understanding are most likely. The intense and profound effect of psychological, biological and neurological symptoms they endure can be devastating. Along with the many social aspects of the ongoing trauma effects has on individuals. Listening intently is the proper place to start working on the problems and resulting behaviors associated with trauma.

Victims have constant needs for safety and to be heard. It's vital that people around them understand their struggles and the profound ways they learn to connect and cope with daily living.

Our anxiety over another's predicament is uncomfortable for us and so our attempts at fixing others is tied to our need to fix us. We can learn different ways to be present for trauma survivors.

Some of the worst trauma triggers are not being heard and people fight, yell and rage. I will instantly disassociate when in the presence of rage and once drove seven hours without any memory of it after being in an argument with a family member.

Love is so much more efficient if you allow it to work its magic. It gives for the sake of love itself. It's not working to try and fix anything, just remind you of its nature. Love listens and empathizes. It bathes you in warmth as it caresses you gently, soothing you in tender rhythmic waves.

Philippians 4:6-7 NIV
Do not be anxious about anything, but in every situation, by prayer and petition, with thanksgiving, present your requests to God. And the peace of God, which transcends all understanding, will guard your hearts and your minds in Christ Jesus.

Matthew 11:28 NIV
Come to me all you who are weary and burdened, and I will give you rest.

Wisdom of Solomon 16:12 KIV
"For it was neither herbe, nor mollifying plaister that restored them to health: but thy word, O Lord, which healeth all things.

Psalm.119:50-55 KJV

This is my comfort in my affliction: for thy word hath quickened me. The proud have had me greatly in derision: yet have I not declined from thy law. I remembered the judgments of old, O Lord; and have comforted myself. Horror hath taken hold upon me because of the wicked that forsake thy law. Thy statutes have been my songs in the house of my pilgrimage. I have remembered thy name, O Lord, in the night, and have kept thy law.

TRUSTING AND ACCEPTING LOVE

Not everyone is capable of trusting love. Traumatic experiences connected to love or those entrusted to love us, are not technically loved by any stretch of the imagination. This can leave one weak and vulncrable. Easily lacking trust when love enters into your world.

Without trust one does not fully commit to a relationship and tends to self-sabotage. This is much like a test. If I'm truly loved even when my behavior is counterproductive and bad for the relationship, then that must be true love. In fact, it's not even close.

Jesus came so that each of us could know and understand Him in a personal way, and to end our sin dilemma by dying on the cross. Jesus alone can bring meaning and understanding about true love as well as our purpose and purpose to our life. He has a definite plan and purpose in mind for each of us.

What keeps us from knowing God intimately? Deep down, our attitude may be one of active rebellion or passive indifference toward God and His ways. This is all evidence of what the Bible refers to as sin.

Sin is like a virus. A virus infects people by injecting parts of itself into our good cells. Sin is a spiritual virus that infects every part of our lives. It leaves us spiritually weak.

James 1:15

And when sin is allowed to grow, it gives birth to death". Sin is like a virus. Sin is rebellion, indifference or simply not caring. This keeps us at arm's length from Christ and can keep us from loving God.

The result of sin in our lives is death and spiritual separation from God. Although we may try to get close to God through our own effort, it is not possible, and we inevitably fail. God calls us to Him, we do not call ourselves to God.

Proverbs 3:5 NIV

Trust in the Lord with all your heart, and do not lean on your own understanding.

Psalm 118:8 NIV

It is better to take refuge in the LORD than to trust in man.

Psalm 46:10 NIV

He says, "Be still, and know that I am God. I will be exalted among the nations; I will be exalted in the earth!"

Psalm 28:7 NASB-1995

The LORD is my strength and my shield; My heart trusts in Him, and I am helped; Therefore, my heart exults, And with my song I shall thank Him.

There is a distance and gap between us and God. We might try and reach God by our own efforts such as doing good works for others, adopting religious rituals, and trying to be a good person, etc. A problem exists in that none of these good works actually cover up our sin or remove it from us. We are sinners to the core with no ability to free or save ourselves.

Our sin is known by God and can be a stumbling block between us and Him. The Bible explains this in-depth, and we are reminded that the penalty for sin is death. Sin can create a chasm of eternal separation from God if we do not love the Lord in return for His sacrificial love for us.

God, out of His enormous love, sacrificed His only Son so that we might have eternal life.

John 15:9-17 NIV

"This is my commandment, that you love one another as I have loved you. No one has greater love than this, to lay down one's life for one's friends. You are my friends if you do what I command you.

So what do we need to do to have a relationship with God? Surrender and give us over to Christ's love.

To surrender to God is to freely give up his own will and subject his thoughts, ideas, and deeds to the will and teachings of a higher power. It may also be submitting oneself. To surrender is willful acceptance and yielding to a dominating force and their own will.

Surrendering to God is extremely difficult for many, especially in light of the reality that the battle has already been lost. We often evade being captured by God because it's so hard to let go of areas of our lives we want to control. Deciding who is going to take possession of the throne and determine our destiny is a genuine struggle of biblical proportions. To live the life that God has planned for us which He promises is best, requires humbly throwing in the towel and surrendering to our creator.

Romans 8:28 KJV

And we know that all things work together for good to those who love God, who are called according to his purpose.

How can we accomplish surrender? In God's Word, Jesus Christ gives us detailed instructions on how to do this.

Matthew 16:24-25 NIV

Then Jesus said to his disciples, "Whoever wants to be my disciple must deny themselves and take up their cross and follow me. For whoever wants to save their life will lose it, but whoever loses their life for me will find it.

The hardest step is being open to the process of surrendering. Christ's invitation to join Him is subtle and an open invitation to surrender.

The invitation being a glorious walk through life with the creator of the universe who is Savior to all sinners and who accepted death on the cross for all each of us.

As exciting as that sounds, it is not so easy to do. It is contrary to our stubborn and sinful hearts. For the non-believer it requires admitting that you are a sinner in need of a Savior. It takes embracing Jesus Christ by faith and receiving loving eternal grace, which allows a person to surrender in the first place. For some, it can take years.

If you are already a believer, your Christian walk reveals that you have the greatest advocate and friend you will ever have, found in Jesus Christ.

1 John 2:1-2 KJV

My little children, these things write I unto you, that ye sin not. And if any man sin, we have an advocate with the Father, Jesus Christ the righteous: and he is the propitiation for our sins: and not for our's only, but also for the sins of the whole world.

God has specific expectations for each of us for our good, along with conditions to follow. After you've decided to surrender, you must then deny yourself, surrendering your self-will and accepting God's perfect will. This can be daunting. Give some thought for a moment to whose terms you're living by, yours or God's?

Jeremiah 10:23 AMP

O LORD, I know that the path of a man is not in himself; It is not within man to choose and direct his steps.

What does it mean to take up God's cross? As believers, we know that we are crucified with Christ on the cross but that Jesus paid the price for our sins for all of mankind. The crucifixion gives us the opportunity to fellowship with Him for eternity. We share in the burden of carrying the cross and are to seek God's will for us at all cost.

Galatians 2:20 NIV

I have been crucified with Christ and I no longer live, but Christ lives in me. The life I now live in the body, I live by faith in the Son of God, who loved me and gave himself for.

2 Timothy 1:7 KJV

For God hath not given us the spirit of fear; but of power, and of love, and of a sound mind.

Lastly, we are to follow Christ in our surrender. Jesus invited Andrew and Peter to follow him and they left everything behind to do so. It is tough to be a follower because we like being the leader. We are impatient and want to move ahead at our own speed. We often feel that God is moving to slowly thus reviving the tug of war for control of the throne again. When we proceed on our own, we leave the safety of His will for the uncertainty of our own.

Being a dedicated follower of Christ requires wisdom and strength but most assuredly the ability to surrender control and exist within the parameters of God's will for us.

Find your life. Simply put, anyone seeking to save their own life by chasing their own interests and rejecting God's free gift of Jesus Christ, will inherit instead a shallow, meaningless life away from Him for eternity. Those who reject Him, have no hope or place in Heaven.

To surrender to Jesus God's Son is the most important decision a person can make. May God bless you with the perfect choice.

Proverbs 23:36 KJV

My son, give me thine heart, and let thine eyes observe my ways.

Jesus Christ upon His death on the cross, paid the penalty for our sin for us. He took our sins unto Himself and now offers us complete forgiveness and an intimate relationship with him.

Jesus chose death on our behalf. He took our place and died for us out of his enormous love for His people.

Christ chose to save us, not because of any righteous things we may have done, but because of His mercy. As a result of Jesus' death on the cross, our sin no longer has to separate us from God.

John 3:16 KJ

"For God so loved the world that he gave his only Son, so that everyone whosoever believeth on him should not perish but have eternal life.

People often reference the term "Find God?" But He's not lost. To know God, read His Word. The Word teaches us about who He is. "Help God." God does not need our help with anything. Or "know God." God sent His only Son Jesus, who not only died for our sin, but after this death on the cross, physically came back to life three days later, just as He said He would. God's Word tells us who He is.

Christ's death on the cross was the final proof that everything Jesus said about himself was true. To know Him is to know God; to love Him is to love God.

Jesus said He could answer prayer, forgive sin, judge the world, give us eternal life. His countless miracles supported His words.

John 14:6 NIV

Jesus was clear; Jesus answered, "I am the way and the truth and the life. No one comes to the Father except through me."

Instead of trying to reach God, He tells us how we can begin a relationship with him right now. Jesus says;

John 7:37 NIV

Whoever believes in me, as Scripture has said, rivers of living water will flow from within them.

It was Jesus' love for us that caused him to endure the cross. And He now invites us to come to Him, that we might begin a personal relationship with Christ.

Just knowing what Jesus has done for us and what he is offering us is not enough. To have a relationship with God, we need to welcome him into our life…study His Word provided to us in the Bible.

God does not require us to accept Him only in a church. There is a process of individually accepting Jesus Christ as Savior and Lord and with it, His love. We accomplish this by opening our hearts and minds to Him. We are each individually chosen and cherished by God. Embrace Him.

Our initial relationship with God or possible relationship difficulties with Him, can stem from our relationship with our earthly father and family. If we experienced trauma, abuse, or abandonment from our earthly father, it might be easy to question God's love or even question why God allowed abuses to occur. The Bible responds with.

John 1:12 NIV
"Yet to all who received him, to those who believed in his name, he gave the right to become children of God."

Ephesians 2:8 KJV
We accept Jesus by God-given faith. The Bible.

For by grace are ye saved through faith; and that not of yourselves: it is the gift of God: not of works, lest any man should boast.

Accepting Jesus as your Savior means believing that Jesus is the Son of God, allowing Him by invitation to guide and direct our lives.

John 10:10 KJV
The thief cometh not, but for to steal, and to kill, and to destroy: "I am come that they might have life, and that they might have it more abundantly."

Jesus offered us a direct invitation and He could not have been any clearer. Jesus offers a reliable relationship with Him and wants us to know the depth of His love for His people.

Revelation 3:20 NIV
Here I am! I stand at the door and knock. If anyone hears my voice and opens the door, I will come in and eat with that person, and they with me.

What has your response to God's invitation been like? Have you responded at all? Are you uncertain or need more information or persuasion? How is God likely to swing your vote in the direction of a never-ending true and authentic love? You have nothing to lose by accepting the invitation to a life of freedom and security in Christ's love. To accept the invitation is to simply place your God-given faith, in Him.

God offers the free gift of salvation with His offer of love. He asks that you believe that Jesus died on the cross as payment for your sins.

Ephesians 4:1-6 NIV

As a prisoner for the Lord, then, I urge you to live a life worthy of the calling you have received. Be completely humble and gentle; be patient, bearing one another in love. Make every effort to keep the unity of the Spirit through the bond of peace. There is one body and one Spirit, just as you were called to one hope when you were called; one Lord, one faith, one baptism; one God and Father of all, who is over all and through all and in all.

FinDing GoDs Love

Y ou may have found God and consequently His love, but God found you and has pursued you from the womb. Each of us is presented with the opportunity to surrender ourselves to the Lord. He wants all His people to face forward to Him.

Surrendering to God can be extremely difficult for people to socially in light of the reality that the battle has already been lost. We often evade being captured by God because it's so hard to let go of the areas of our lives we want to control. Deciding who is going to take possession of the throne and determine our destiny is a genuine struggle of biblical proportions. To live the life that God has planned for us which He promises is best, requires humbly throwing in the towel and surrendering to our creator.

Romans 8:28 NIV

And we know that in all things God works for the good of those who love him, who have been called according to his purpose.

How can we surrender to God and in the process discover His great love for us? In God's Word, Jesus Christ gives us detailed instructions on how to accomplish this.

Matthew 16:24-25 NIV

Then Jesus said to his disciples, "Whoever wants to be my disciple must deny themselves and take up their cross and follow me. For whoever wants to save their life[a] will lose it, but whoever loses their life for me will find it.

Should you surrender? Absolutely! In Matthew passages, there is an outline and challenge for the necessary steps for surrender.

- Be open to surrender.
- Deny yourself.
- Take up God's cross.
- Follow Him.

The hardest step is being open to the process of surrendering. Christ's invitation to join Him is subtle and an open invitation. The invitation is a glorious walk-through life with the creator of the universe who is not only Savior to all sinners but died on the cross for all sinners.

As exciting as those sounds, it is not so easy to do. It is contrary to our stubborn and sinful hearts. For the non-believer, it requires admitting that you are a sinner in need of a Savior. It takes embracing Jesus Christ by faith and receiving loving eternal grace, which allows a person to surrender in the first place. For some, it can take years.

If you are already a believer, your Christian walk reveals that you have the greatest advocate and friend you will ever have, found only in Jesus Christ.

1 John 2:1 ESV

Do not love the world or the things in the world. If anyone loves the world, the love of the Father is not in him.

God has specific expectations and plans for each of us for our own individual good, along with conditions to follow. After you've decided to surrender, you must then deny yourself, surrendering your self-will and accepting God's perfect will. This can be daunting. Give some thought for a moment to whose terms you're living by, yours or God's?

Jeremiah 10:23 AMP

O LORD, I know that the path of a man is not in himself; It is not within [the limited ability of] man [even one at his best] to choose and direct his steps.

What does it mean to take up God's cross? As believers, we know that we are crucified with Christ on the cross but that Jesus paid the price for our sins for all of mankind. The crucifixion gives us the opportunity to fellowship with Him for eternity. We share in the burden of carrying the cross and are to seek God's will for us in everything we can do.

Galatians 2:20 NIV

I have been crucified with Christ and I no longer live, but Christ lives in me. The life I now live in the body, I live by faith in the Son of God, who loved me and gave himself for me.

2 Timothy 1:7 KJV

For God hath not given us the spirit of fear; but of power, and of love, and of a sound mind.

Lastly, we are to "follow" Christ as we surrender to Him. Jesus invited Andrew and Peter to follow him and they left everything behind to do so. It is tough to follow because we like being in the lead. We are impatient and want to move ahead at our own speed. We often feel that God is moving to slowly or not at all thus reviving the tug of war for control of the throne again. When we proceed on our own, we leave the safety of His will for the uncertainty of our own.

Being a dedicated follower of Christ requires wisdom and strength but most assuredly the ability to surrender control and exist within the parameters of God's will for us.

Find your life. Simply put, anyone seeking to save their own life by chasing their own interests and rejecting God's free gift of Jesus Christ, will inherit instead a shallow, meaningless life away from God for eternity. Those who reject Him, have no hope or place in Heaven.

To surrender to Jesus God's Son is the most important decision a person can make. May God bless you with the perfect choice. A decision for eternal life everlasting.

Proverbs 23:26 KJV

My son, give me your heart and let thine eyes observe my ways.

God does not ever give up on us or throw in the towel as He pursues us. If you were born and raised in a Christian home dedicated to worshipping Christ, you were blessed with knowledge of Christ's love and devotion to you. You still made a decision as an adult to accept or reject the Lord.

Those raised outside of the Christian community sometimes need more work depending on their life circumstances. Nonetheless God in His Holiness wanted you. And He doesn't give up or back down.

You don't have to go anywhere to find God's love. His desire is for you to know love and accept it freely, right where you are.

The only way to love others harder is to first accept God's love for yourself. Love causes us and helps us to reach outside ourselves and build relationships and encourage others. To that end, we bless those around us.

LOVE IMPOSTORS

Consider this scenario:

Find God, get to know God and with that knowledge live a self-directed life. This particular scenario is in essence helping you to the throne.

A self-directed life will lead you to discord and endless frustrations. Jesus then becomes outside your life as you have not surrendered to God's will and direction for you.

To find and know God is to allow for and welcome a Christ-directed life. Jesus then becomes part of your daily living, directing your days. Jesus is in your life and operating from His glorious throne.

Having accepted a life in Christ, you now begin a meaningful relationship with a God-directed purpose. One can now experience a directional, useful, and committed relationship with God. We accomplish that through God's love, guidance, and daily help as we walk in a centered relationship with God. By daily living and seeking Him in all things.

Keep in mind some people, during difficult trials, will encounter imposters. A trial in life doesn't have to exist for this phenomenon to occur.

2 Timothy 3:13-17 NIV

While evildoers and impostors will go from bad to worse, deceiving and being deceived. But as for you, continue in what you have learned and have become convinced of, because you know those from whom you learned it, and how from infancy you have known the Holy Scriptures, which are able to make you wise for salvation through faith in Christ Jesus. All Scripture is God-breathed and is useful for teaching, rebuking, correcting, and training in righteousness, so that the servant of God[a] may be thoroughly equipped for every good work.

We have many emotions, some of which become idols and impostors. Power and control and the need it feeds is a deceitful feeling of love when recognized. It is primarily acting out of fear and doesn't honor other people's freedom. The truth is it's important to also love and empower yourself, existing in God's holy realm. It is freeing to recognize our strengths.

Sacrifice is another way to be honored. However, there isn't a positive outcome for being a martyr. You will ultimately always come in last place, as you deplete your emotional stores. The truth is when you prioritize you actually re-energize yourself and God is better able to use you as a compassionate servant.

Being a caretaker and people pleaser creates dependency and doesn't allow others to live independent empowered lives. In the extreme, caretaking and people-pleasing become acts of selfishness, leaving God on the sidelines. Truth is love is a way of watching after ourselves too.

Overly relying on another person can often be confused with love. It too is a form of control and prevents us from learning what our strengths are. The truth is that loving relationships are interdependent not fully dependent which excludes God from the picture.

Unless there is a pressing emergency, rescuing is something we do for ourselves, not others. Being a rescuer and/or fixer also puts you in a victim role. Your self-worth comes from being a hero. Truth is rescuing yourself and leaving others to rescue themselves with God's help and guidance is freedom, not bondage.

Guilt is another emotion and is not connected to love at all. Acting out of guilt is acting out of deep-seeded inadequacies. Thoughts such as "I have to" and "I should" are guilt-laden phrases. Truth is "I'd love to" are empowering phrase pleasing to God as a loving servant.

Charm and idolization are placing people or things on a pedestal. This practice inevitably leads to disappointment. The truth is that love allows us to relate to others in a more honest fashion.

Perfection is the belief that we ourselves or others must behave perfectly in order to be lovable. In reality, the more we can love our flaws and the flaws of others the more we are actually loving harder.

Needing love is more than just desiring love. Desiring love is "I'd like to have love." Needing love sometimes results in us pushing love away. God is considerate of your needs and wants as it is God's way of growing you into one of His beloved.

All in all, God knows our hearts intimately. In fact, we are inept students of our own predicaments and genuinely in need of God's input and guidance in life. Fortunately, we have a loving, considerate Father looking out for us.

Jeremiah 29:11 KJV

For I know the thoughts that I think toward you, saith the Lord, thoughts of peace, and not of evil, to give you an expected end.

It is so reassuring that God has a plan in place for us and it's a better plan than we could ever conceive or carry out ourselves.

A CHOICE FOR LOVE

At anytime, we can choose to accept or reject love. We can make the same decision about Christ. However "choosing" to love Christ sounds like we have special powers to perform. Often the "choice" to love may not be setting the bar high enough. It seems if you have always treated someone well, it unfortunately does not mean you are fully loving them. There are a variety of reasons why this happens. Trust me when I say, people know when they are not being fully loved.

Revelations 3:20 NIV

Behold, I stand at the door, and knock: if any man hear my voice, and opens the door, I will come in to him, and will sup with him, and he with me.

There is no perfect or precise way to commit yourself to God. Words are not as important to the process because God knows your heart's intentions and desires. If you are unsure of how to word things, seek His guidance and speak plainly from your heart. God lives in your heart and hears your hearts desires.

If you begin your conversations with thanks and gratitude, you will not go wrong. Ask God to search your heart and seek His forgiveness and embrace the unearned gift of unconditional love.

Be thankful for a plan from God uniquely designed with you in mind. A plan you could not possibly design or put into action on your own.

You are loved so deeply that God's hand is squarely on you and He is not about to let go.

Isaiah 41:10 ESV

Fear not, for I am with you; be not dismayed, for I am your God; I will strengthen you, I will help you, I will uphold you with my righteous right hand.

Thank God for His hand squarely on you and acknowledging your our daily blessings. Even when life seems difficult, challenging and/or painful, we are never alone. God is faithfully by our side.

You are God's beloved child. He takes His relationship with you seriously, with sincerity and pride. You are His creation. Jesus alone can bring meaning and purpose to your life. Only God can teach and infuse the proper skills needed to equip you in a world with millions of people needing to be loved harder.

Buried beneath our will with many decisions to make, we have a heart that contributes to producing our preferences for things. Use your God given gifts in your effort to love harder.

2 Corinthians 9:7 ESV

"Each one must give as he has decided in his heart, not reluctantly or under compulsion, for God loves a cheerful giver.

When we choose a life with Christ He will listen to the desires of our heart and grant us those desires providing they are within His will and plan for us. Every petition and prayer we place before God is answered. Not every answer is what we asked for though. God does say no from time to time.

Psalm 37:3-4 NIV

Trust in the Lord and do good; dwell in the land and enjoy safe pasture. Take delight in the Lord, and he will give you the desires of your heart.

ℒove ⅅeⅇteⱤⱤents

I saiah 53:6 NIV
    We all, like sheep, have gone astray, each of us has turned to our own way; and the Lord has laid on him the iniquity of us all.

Sin separates us from Christ. Along with our rebellious nature and cultured indifference towards God. Ongoing active and passive rebellion is evidence of our sin nature.

The penalty for our sin is death and the loss of spiritual connection to God. Our own attempts to get close to or reconnect to God will inevitably fail. When a chasm forms and the gap widens between us and God, our attempts to get closer to God simply won't work.

No amount of good works, trying to be good or any religious rituals can save us from ourselves. Our sin is a genuine barrier that keeps us from God's presence. We cannot hide, ignore or cover up our sin.

There are some practical ways we can learn to serve the Lord. Here are a few:

*Cast your cares to the Lord,
*Read God's Word everyday.
*Walk in obedience to God.
*Find your security and confidence in Him alone.

Ways we find ourselves separated from God and we may not feel His love. This is generally a result of sin. When we are deep into our sinful nature should we just continue to sin, hoping for an increased dose of grace? That is not a productive plan. We must face our sin and face Christ, seeking His forgiveness.

As children baptized into Christ Jesus, we also became baptized into Christ's death. Christ was buried and raised from the dead through God's great glory so that we too would have new life.

As a deterrent to love, our emotions and impure thoughts can steer us away from Christ, making it hard to know and comprehend His abiding love for us. Satan has many ways to distract us from Gods love.

Genesis 39:9 NIV

No one is greater in this house than I am. My master has withheld nothing from me except you, because you are his wife. How then could I do such a wicked thing and sin against God.

Job 31:1 NIV

"I made a covenant with my eyes not to look lustfully at a young woman.

Sin finds us everywhere, when we least expect it. We must be on guard at all times against the enemy who takes great pleasure in our downfall. We cannot let him win against us or credit him with any successes.

ULTiMaTe Love

U ltimate love is the most extreme love imaginable, the highest and furthest degree of love possible. A love so great it not fathomable. It is the strongest emotion one can receive. The ultimate sacrifice accomplished on the cross for our salvation. It is the love God has for us.

Ultimate love is the final destination and a series of progressions that can be expressed in several different ways. Through gifts, acts, time, touch and words. The deepest expression of ultimate love can be:

I want you.
I cherish you.
I adore you.
I need you.

We would be eternally separated from God if it weren't for His amazing gift of forgiveness offered unto death on the cross of His only

Son Jesus Christ. Without this generous and sacrificial gift, we would be forever separated from Him. That is an expression of ultimate love.

We are sinful. That is the very thing that keeps us separated from Christ and what Christ died on the cross to save us from. That was ultimate love for us and the cure for our sin problem.

The majority of us become better people with love. Ultimate love causes one to continually think upon the one who loves them. They attribute all the good in their lives to ultimate love. It is an overwhelming, undeniable constant presence. We have that love, freely given and wholly undeserved by Christ our Savior.

You may wonder why would God create us to have sin instead of creating us to be perfect? While I am not going to pretend that I'm an expert at knowing the mind of Christ, I think the answer to the question is love. God desires a love relationship with His people, provided to us for free, not programmed in us. We surrender to God because we first were chosen.

God the Father chose us before the creation of the world to be holy and blameless in His sight. We were created and blessed with every spiritual blessing.

Ephesians 2:8-9 NIV

For it is by grace you have been saved, through faith—and this is not from yourselves, it is the gift of God— not by works, so that no one can boast.

Ephesians 1:3 NIV

Praise be to the God and Father of our Lord Jesus Christ, who has blessed us in the heavenly realms with every spiritual blessing in Christ.

God loves us, even though we are undeserving of that love. And in spite of that fact, His love continues. He could have created us all the same, obedient and sinless but He wants us to love Him back with genuine love and joy. If we were programmed to blindly love God and there was know free will, how could that love be real? There is no reason to believe a robot's reaction because they are built to respond in a definitive way. There is no free will or free thinking involved.

Do you want to be loved by choice or by design? I anticipate that most of God's children want love that chose us and continues to choose us everyday. That counts us blessed by choice.

John 3:16 ESV

"For God so loved the world, that he gave his only Son, that whoever believes in him should not perish but have eternal life."

To know Christ is to know God. To love God is to love Christ. Jesus forgave sin, answered prayers, could judge the entire world and give us eternal life. He performed miracle after miracle to support the validity of who he was, the Son of God. His words were not empty promises.

John 14:6 KJV

Jesus said to him, "I am the way and the truth and the life. No one comes to the Father except through me."

We are not expected to reach God. God explains in His Word how to forge a relationship with Him who is already with us.

John 7:37 KJV

On the last day, that great day of the feast, Jesus stood and cried out, saying, "If anyone thirsts, let him come to Me and drink."

We are to live our lives with the knowledge that no greater love created us and forever pursues us and desires us. We are His creation, intimately known and ultimately loved.

LOVE TRIUMPHANT

It was Jesus' love for us that caused him to endure the cross. And He now invites us to come to him, that we might begin a personal relationship with God.

Just knowing what Jesus has done for us and what he is offering us is not enough. We need to have a relationship with God, welcoming Him into our life.

Accepting Jesus by faith means believing that Jesus is the Son of God, then seeking His guidance and direction in our lives. God saves us so that we cannot claim any credit for it. It is a gift from God not a reward for anything good we may have done. We must not be able to boast about the special gift of Salvation as none of us are capable of earning.

John 1:12 NIV

Yet to all who did receive him, to those who believed in his name, he gave the right to become children of God.

Jesus' offer to us is a genuine heartfelt invitation.

Revelation 3:20 NIV

Here I am! I stand at the door and knock. If anyone hears my voice and opens the door, I will come in and eat with that person, and they with me.

Who is responding to His call and how are His people accepting God's invitation? God's invitation can be accepted by following God's biblical instructions.

Acts 2:38 NIV

Peter replied, "Repent and be baptized, every one of you, in the name of Jesus Christ for the forgiveness of your sins. And you will receive the gift of the Holy Spirit."

The appropriate response to God's grace is to also offer yourself as a living sacrifice. Choosing the life of a servant of Christ.

Romans 12:1 NIV

Therefore, I urge you, brothers and sisters, in view of God's mercy, to offer your bodies as a living sacrifice, holy and pleasing to God-this is your true and proper worship.

Romans 8:35-39 NIV

Who shall separate us from the love of Christ? Shall trouble or hardship or persecution or famine or nakedness or danger or sword? As it is written: "For your sake we face death all day long; we are considered as sheep to be slaughtered."

No, in all these things we are more than conquerors through him who loved us. For I am convinced that neither death nor life, neither angels nor demons, neither the present nor the future, nor any powers, neither height nor depth, nor anything else in all creation, will be able to separate us from the love of God that is in Christ Jesus our Lord.

WHATS LOVE GOT TO DO WITH IT?

W hich scenario best represents your life? Are you in it to win it? Sitting on the fence? Waiting anxiously for a reason to move forward or retreat? Scared of your own shadow or too angry to be of any earthly good? This isn't a dress rehearsal. You're in a role, so you may as well choose the role you wish to play instead of getting assigned a role you may not want.

Christ can and will offer you a plan right now. He has sent out the invitation already. He knows the intentions of your heart like no one else does. You can look away from God but you cannot hide from Him.

What does it actually take to begin a relationship with God? Wait for a special spiritual experience? Work tirelessly devoting yourself to unselfish religious deeds? Be a better person so that God will accept you? NONE of these things can persuade God's or bring good favor upon you. God has made it very clear in the Bible how we can know Him.

God, having created you, loves you so much that he wants you to know him now and spend eternity with him. Jesus came so that each of us could know and understand God in a personal way. Only a relationship with Jesus can bring essential meaning and purpose to life.

What keeps us from a relationship with God or knowing Him better? All of us sin and it is our sin that has separated us from God. Daily sin and perpetual sin plague us and our hearts can grow farther away from God by our sin. Relationships gone bad? Living the consequences of dysfunction? Pain from relationship punishments, like the silent treatment? If so, through Christ's death on the cross we have a reprieve.

If you are a victim of the silent treatment as a weapon or are using this technique on others, carefully consider its power and reconsider its use. The silent treatment is not loving anyone harder.

Silence: Be careful to utilize silence judiciously as a strength. Ensure your words carry weight when you choose to speak. Silence is a powerful sword. When used out of love, it can show that we care deeply enough to listen with intent to understand. When used as a weapon to cut people off it is ultimately painful. God's silence is an opportunity to remain faithful, even when you are unsure of His intentions for your life. He is God and we are not. Silence is not empty, it is full of answers. Listen to the silence.

Proverbs 17:28 NKJV
Even a fool who keeps silent is considered wise; when he closes his lips, he is deemed intelligent.

Lamentations 3:28 NKJV
Let him sit alone in silence when it is laid on him.

Isaiah 53:6 NIV
We all, like sheep, have gone astray, each of us has turned to our own way; and the Lord has laid on him the iniquity of us all.

Individually our attitude deep down at the core may be one of active rebellion or passive indifference in relationship to God and his expectations for us. All of which is ongoing evidence that the Bible refers too as sin.

The result of sin in our lives is death – nothing short of spiritual separation from God. We may even try to bridge the "sin" gap on our own but will inevitably fail. We can accomplish no amount of "saving" ourselves under our own power. We are humbly and desperately in need of our Savior Christ.

Our sin is seen and known by God and is the impenetrable barrier between us and God. Further, the Bible states that the penalty for sin is death. We would be eternally separated from God, had Christ not taken our sin upon himself and died on the cross with it. Jesus died for us, in our place out of his tremendous love for us.

Titus 3:5.1 NIV

He saved us, not because of righteous things we had done, but because of his mercy. He saved us through the washing of rebirth and renewal by the Holy Spirit.

Because of Jesus' death on the cross and amazing sacrifice for us, our sin doesn't have to separate us from God any longer.

Death on the cross was the final proof that everything Jesus said about himself was true. To know him was to know God; to love him was to love God.

John 10:30 NIV

"I and the Father are one."

Jesus said he could answer prayer, forgive sin, judge the world and give us eternal life. His countless miracles and servant's heart supported His words.

Jesus continually expressed a servant's heart. He loved and served those around him through healing, teaching, and admonishing, as He walked amongst His people. He has never stopped being a servant to us.

Ephesians 6:7-9 NIV

Serve wholeheartedly, as if you were serving the Lord, not people, because you know that the Lord will reward each one for whatever good they do, whether they are slave or free. And masters, treat your slaves in the same way.

John 14:6 NIV

Jesus answered, "I am the way and the truth and the life. No one comes to the Father except through me."

Instead of trying to reach God on our own, He tells us clearly in the Word, how we can begin a relationship with him right now. So, how does one begin to develop a deeper relationship with God?

*Spend time with Him through prayer and read His word. ...
*Talk to God wherever you are.
*Worship Him always. …
*Practice obedience to His word….
*Be Willing to trust Him with your heart.

John 7:37-38 NIV

On the last and greatest day of the festival, Jesus stood and said in a loud voice, "Let anyone who is thirsty come to me and drink. Whoever believes in me, as Scripture has said, rivers of living water will flow from within them.

Jesus' love for us was so great that He chose to endure the cross, in order to save us from eternal death and suffering. He stands ready and invites us to come to Him, so that we might begin to know Him in a personal and intimate way.

Just having knowledge of what Jesus has done for us and what He is offering us is not enough. Jesus wants a "salvational" ongoing conversation with Him and is His way of welcoming us into a relationship with Him.

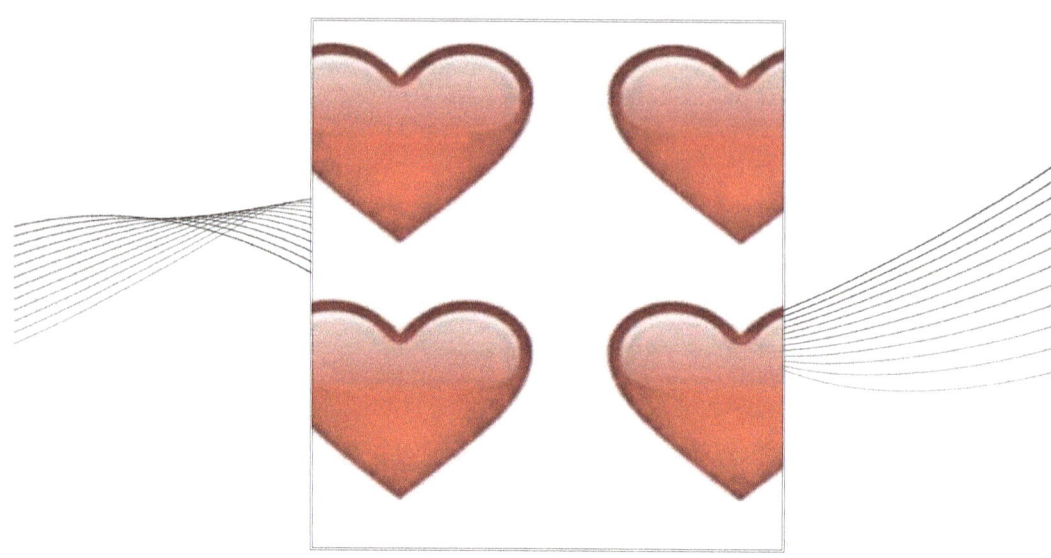

ᒍOᐯᕮ ᗩᑎᗪ ᖴᗩITᕼ

W e accept Jesus through faith.

Romans 10:17

"Faith comes from hearing, and hearing through the word of Christ"

Ephesians 2:8-10 NLT

God saved you by his grace when you believed. And you can't take credit for this; it is a gift from God. Salvation is not a reward for the good things we have done, so none of us can boast about it. For we are God's masterpiece. He has created us anew in Christ Jesus, so we can do the good things he planned for us long ago.

This "word" is ultimately from God, "inspired" and quite literally "breathed out" by God through the work of the Holy Spirit that God has given to us.

To be certain, Jesus is standing at the door knocking. We can begin a relationship with Jesus by answering the door.

It is easy to get trapped into our own fears, concerns and worries. Is it's lack of faith that pulls us into the darkness? Is faith an attitude, positive thinking or just a feeling? Is it simply believing in Christ with confidence and hope? What happens if we have no faith?

Hebrews 11:6 NIV

Instead, they were longing for a better country—a heavenly one. Therefore God is not ashamed to be called their God, for he has prepared a city for them.

When we have faith, we also have trust. Just as we cannot earn love, we cannot earn faith.

Have trust with your entire being that God knows what is best for His people and has us securely in His care. In order to trust what God has planned for each of us, we must "fully" trust. Trust is not foolishness. Our God is faithful and good. His love is sacred and grand.

Life is precious and purposeful. It can also be undeniably difficult on many occasions and for some, continually negatively climactic. Faith comes from God and hearing the Word. It helps us to get through adversity and traumas illuminating times of darkness, helping to provide us strength when we are weak. We are nothing without God given faith.

The Bible gives us an understanding of the Word of God and what fellowship with God is like and a life with Christ produces. Love for God and one another is the very essence, heart, and the fabric of Scripture. These two great commands are at the heart of the rest of God's commands in the Word. The rest of Scripture gives us God's explanation on loving God and loving one another. Scripture provides us with everything required to continue in relationship and communication with Him. It paves the way to a love relationship with Christ and each other.

All other commands and principles of Scripture point us to their meaning and purpose in two main things. Our love for God and love for men, made in the image of God.

We find in the New Testament thirteen times the injunction, "love one another." These injunctions to love one another give us the substance and summary of our responsibility to others.

We learn to love each other in earnest by encouraging them, praying for them, being humble before them, being hospitable and serve others with love. Demonstrate love and forgiveness. Don't badmouth others. Speak the truth to others in love and bear one another's burdens.

Through the filling of the Holy Spirit, fellowship with Christ who dwells within us, and knowing and applying God's Word, we are able to stop making provision for the flesh.

Ephesians 4:21-32 NIV

When you heard about Christ and were taught in him in accordance with the truth that is in Jesus. You were taught, with regard to your former way of life, to put off your old self, which is being corrupted by its deceitful desires; to be made new in the attitude of your minds; and to put on the new self, created to be like God in true righteousness and holiness. Therefore each of you must put off falsehood and speak truthfully to your neighbor, for we are all members of one body. "In your anger do not sin": Do not let the sun go down while you are still angry, and do not give the devil a foothold. Anyone who has been stealing must steal no longer, but must work, doing something useful with their own hands, that they may have something to share with those in need. Do not let any unwholesome talk come out of your mouths, but only what is helpful for building others up according to their needs, that it may benefit those who listen. And do not grieve the Holy Spirit of God, with whom you were sealed for the day of redemption. Get rid of all bitterness, rage and anger, brawling and slander, along with every form of malice. Be kind and compassionate to one another, forgiving each other, just as in Christ God forgave you.

Always love Christ and love one another. Love everyone harder.

If one is without faith, it is impossible to please God. For those who come to God must believe that He is and that He rewards those who seek Him.

God understands us perfectly and knows everything we are going through and what is in our future. He also knows the best way to handle any situation that might arise for us. We can trust the God knows the best possible outcome and we need to trust Him for that. We need to follow the path He has laid out before us.

It can be strenuously difficult to maintain faith under difficult circumstances. Those hard times are when faith is most important. It can be our saving grace.if we loose faith it can always be restored.

Hebrews 11:1 NIV

11 Now faith is confidence in what we hope for and assurance about what we do not see.

What is the appropriate response to God's grace and love? A logical response to God's grace is to offer yourself as a living sacrifice also. Choosing to live a life of grace and sacrifice too.

Romans 12:1 ESV

I appeal to you therefore, brothers,by the mercies of God, ato present your bodies bas a living sacrifice, holy and acceptable to God, which is your spiritual worship. I beseech you therefore, brethren, by the mercies of God, that you present your bodies a living sacrifice, holy, acceptable to God, which is your spiritual worship.

When we are seeking glory from one another, it hinders our capacity. It affects our ability to trust in God's acceptance and evaluation of our lives. Such a trust causes us to seek from men what only God can give us. When we are searching from men, validation of who we are, we are seeking our security and sense of significance from men's praise, applause, and approval, rather than resting by faith in God's promises of His Word.

Ultimately, the glory from God is found only in Jesus Christ, and it is through Christ that men find security, and significance as citizens in the world. Not only must we come to Christ for God's righteousness, but we must learn to rest in God's acceptance and evaluation of who we are in His Beloved, the Lord Jesus.

Ephesians 1:6 KJV

To the praise of the glory of his grace, wherein he hath made us accepted in the beloved.

John 1:12 KJV

But as many as received him, to them gave he power to become the sons of God, even to them that believe on His name.

Ephesians 2:10 NLT

"For we are God's masterpiece. He has created us anew in Christ Jesus, so we can do the good things he planned for us long ago."

Ephesians 1:6 NLT

So we praise God for the glorious grace he has poured out on us who belong to his dear son.

In Christ our sins are removed and we find complete acceptance. We become accepted in the Beloved.

John 1:12-13 KJV

But as many as received him, to them gave he power to become the sons of God, even to them that believe on his name: which were born, not of blood, nor of the will of the flesh, nor of the will of man, but of God.

Love and Negative Commands

Negative commands help us to understand the hindrances to loving one another and hindrances to fellowship with others. These negative injunctions stress and point to what we naturally tend to do as sinners without a life of Christ. Or without the life-changing power of the Lord, the ministry of the Holy Spirit, and the renewal of our hearts in God's daily Word.

Some examples of God's negative commands are here as follows;

Romans 14:13 KJV

"Let us not therefore judge one another any more: but judge this rather, that no man put a stumbling block or an occasion to fall in his brother's way.

1 Corinthians 6:7 NLT

Even to have such lawsuits with one another is a defeat for you. Why not just accept the injustice and leave it at that? Why not let yourselves be cheated?

Galatians 5:15 NIV

If you bite and devour one another, watch out or you'll be devoured by each other.

Galatians 5:26 NIV

Let us not become conceited, provoking and envying each other.

James 4:11-12 NKJV

Do not speak evil of one another, brethren. He who speaks evil of a brother and judges his brother, speaks evil of the law and judges the law. But if you judge the law, you are not a doer of the law but a judge. There is one Lawgiver, who is able to save and to destroy.

James 5:9 NIV

Don't grumble against one another, brothers and sisters, or you will be judged. The Judge is standing at the door!

John 5:44 KJV

How can ye believe, which receive honor one of another, and seek not the honor that cometh from God only?

It is tremendously important to the entire process of surrendering to God, that in order to love one another we must adhere to these commands. We cannot disregard their importance to the unbelievers in the world. It is easy to miss the purpose of God's Word.

Failure to see our sinfulness, is a fundamental failure to see the need of the cross and the suffering Savior whose death saved us from eternal separation from God.

Failure to see our sinfulness and weaknesses, continues to reinforce the notion that there isn't a need for Christ at all. What we do in our lives is for our own glory and for admiration and praise from the world. This recognition is self-love.

John 5:42 ESV

But I know that you do not have the love of God within you. But I know you. I know you do not have the love of God in your hearts.

John 5:44 MSG

How do you expect to get anywhere with God when you spend all your time jockeying for position with each other, ranking your rivals and ignoring God?

How do we appropriately respond to God's grace and love? The most logical response to God's glorious grace is offering yourself as a servant in the world and as a living sacrifice.

Romans 12:1 NIV

Therefore, I urge you, brothers and sisters, in view of God's mercy, to offer your bodies as a living sacrifice, holy and pleasing to God—this is your true and proper worship.

Without awareness and recognition of our sinfulness and need, without faith in God's Son and the cross, without truly resting in who we are in Christ and His acceptance of us, we are left to justify ourselves and find our sense of security and significance of our lives from each other. Seeking glory from one another instead of Christ causes an inability to love one another according to God's Word.

Failing to understand the character of God's Word, it is easy to become engrossed with our own performance and appearance. It becomes significant to look good, perform well and be important. Being self-righteous will blind us to our ultimate goal to love God and love.

Love and Grace

We were each created and loved into existence and thrive on God's Grace and Mercy. There is evidence from the two great commandments and the many commands to love one another a clear mark of maturity. A mature man or woman walking in obedience to God, will be more likely the ones who love generously. Not seeking to love some people less.

People must choose to act against naturally occurring unloving inclinations and feelings towards others. In our daily walk with God a deeper love should occur as we become more like Christ through God's Word.

Why do we so often fail to love or just fail at love? Because we are seeking glory from men instead of through reliance on the Lord. We are unfortunately looking to get from people what only the Lord can and longs to give.

We sometimes build walls of protection around ourselves for, but these walls will ultimately become hindrances to our ability to love and serve one another.

Walls are built up as a result of abuse and/or dysfunction and trauma. Often when seeking God, our vision of Him will resemble the earthly father we were given. We must grow past this false image of God and through God's Word come to accept what scripture tells us about God. Even though it is just a glimpse, God is providing daily evidence of His deep love for us.

Romans 5:1-2 NIV

Therefore, since we have been justified through faith, we have peace with God through our Lord Jesus Christ, 2 through whom we have gained access by faith into this grace in which we now stand. And we boast in the hope of the glory of God.

Grace is obtained "through Jesus." We literally are too "stand"" in the grace of God. Grace received though not earned. By this we are saved by grace.

Ephesians 2:8-9 NIV

For it is by grace you have been saved, through faith—and this is not from yourselves, it is the gift of God—not by works, so that no one can boast.

God has supplied us grace. We must then learn to stand firm in it. We do this in order to grow in grace which is multiplied.

2 Peter 3:18 NIV

But grow in the grace and knowledge of our Lord and Savior Jesus Christ. To him be glory both now and forever! Amen.

We are not told to grow beyond it but to grow in it, standing firm. Grace and peace are multiplied by God. An amazing concept. Mercy is not getting something you do deserve and Grace is getting something you do deserve. The "somethings" referred to are generally referred to as salvation and judgement.

1 Peter 4:10 NIV

Each of you should use whatever gift you have received to serve others, as faithful stewards of God's grace in its various forms.

1 Peter 5:5 NKJV

Likewise you younger people, submit yourselves to your elders. Yes, all of you be submissive to one another, and be clothed with humility, for God resists the proud,

But gives grace to the humble.

It is our sin that separates us from God. Without a savior left on our own, we deserve to end hopeless and in hell. Mercy is not going to hell. Grace is receiving salvation and life eternal even though we are hopeless sinners.

Thankfully delight in God's grace.

LOVE IN THE GARDEN

There is no current Garden of Eden where we can live a life of perfection. Christ is no longer walking the earth performing miracles. He is however with us and miracles still abound. It is important to be actively engaged in this life and cling to Christ daily.

There is much sadness and pain in this world but thankfully we have a Heavenly Father who will never abandon us. We are surrounded by evil and are victims to evil circumstances at times. Our Bible study and worship habits will help us stay connected to our Lord.

Try pursuing Christ with a deep thirst and hunger. Be passionate about God's Word. Reach out with love and compassion along with a spirit of hospitality to all those around us.

Do not seek personal glory, security and special recognition from this life but gain your identity in Christ the Savior. As long as we seek from man, what only God can provide through Christ, we will not be utilizing faith in the Only one who can fill our empty sack. That is the most fundamental need, knowing God and missing the mark by searching in all the wrong places with the wrong notions and incorrect tools for finding Him.

We must seek His kingdom and His righteousness to know and rest in Him and permanently retire our earthly longings and needs to the Lord.

Matthew 6:33 NIV

But seek first his kingdom and his righteousness, and all these things will be given to you as well.

Matthew 6:31 NIV

So do not worry, saying, 'What shall we eat?' or 'What shall we drink?' or 'What shall you wear."

Matthew 6:32 NKJV

For after all these things the Gentiles seek. For your heavenly Father knows that you need all these things.

Matthew 6:34. NIV

Therefore do not worry about tomorrow, for tomorrow will worry about itself. Each day has enough trouble of its own.

These scriptural exhortations deal with our improper longings, involving our relationships with people ,when we've lost our sense of direction and our focus is no longer on God's kingdom.

Matthew 7:1-5 NIV

"Do not judge, or you too will be judged. For in the same way you judge others, you will be judged, and with the measure you use, it will be measured to you. "Why do you look at the speck of sawdust in your brother's eye and pay no attention to the plank in your own eye? How can you say to your brother, 'Let me take the speck out of your eye,' when all the time there is a plank in your own eye? You hypocrite, first take the plank out of your own eye, and then you will see clearly to remove the speck from your brother's eye.

In other words, go for God first. Get your own life in order before Him. God is not your last resort, He is your first hope. Then submit to God's authority and you will have the ability to truly deal with people from a love stance. Loving others harder than you could of your own accord.

SURRENDERING TOO LOVE

Surrendering to God is extremely difficult for many, especially in light of the reality that the battle has already been lost. We often evade being captured by God because it's so hard to let go of areas of our lives we want to control. Deciding who is going to take possession of the throne and determine your destiny is a genuine struggle of biblical proportions.

To let go and let God, to coin an over used expression, is still none the less pertinent and helpful. How to acknowledge God and relinquish nagging doubts and give over your life to God alone is the question to answer.

God is ALWAYS in complete control over every aspect of our lives. To really live the life that God has planned for us which He promises is best, requires humbly throwing in the towel and surrendering to our creator. Much of the reasoning behind why some people can't readily turn over their lives to God I'd because they no God on a limited basis. it is possible and preferable to turn over all your cares and worries to. God.

Romans 8:28 NLT

And we know that God causes everything to work together[a] for the good of those who love God and are called according to his purpose for them.

How can we accomplish surrendering? In God's Word, Jesus Christ gives us detailed instructions on how to do this.

Matthew 16:24-25 NLT

Then Jesus said to his disciples, "If any of you wants to be my follower, you must give up your own way, take up your cross, and follow me. If you try to hang on to your life, you will lose it. But if you give up your life for my sake, you will save it."

Should you surrender? Absolutely! In Matthews passage there is an outline and challenge for the necessary steps for surrender.

- Be open to surrender.
- Deny yourself.
- Take up God's cross.
- Follow Him.

The hardest step is being open to the process of surrendering. Christ's invitation to join Him is subtle and an open invitation to surrender. The invitation being a glorious walk through life with the creator of the universe who is not only the Savior to all sinners but died on the cross for all sinners.

As exciting as that sounds, it is not so easy to do. It is contrary to our stubborn and sinful hearts. For the non-believer it requires admitting that you are a sinner in need of a Savior. It takes embracing Jesus Christ by faith and receiving loving eternal grace, which allows a person to surrender in the first place. For some, it can take years.

If you are already a believer, your Christian walk reveals that you have the greatest Advocate and Friend you will ever have, found in Jesus Christ.

1 John 2:1 NIV

My dear children, I write this to you so that you will not sin. But if anybody does sin, we have an advocate with the Father—Jesus Christ, the Righteous One.

God has specific expectations for each of us for our good, along with conditions to follow. After you've decided to surrender, you must then deny yourself, surrendering your self-will and accepting God's perfect will. This can be daunting. Give some thought for a moment to whose terms you're living by, yours or God's?

Jeremiah 10:23 AMP

O LORD, I know that the path of [life of] a man is not in himself; It is not within man to choose and direct his steps.

What does it mean to take up God's cross? As believers, we know that we are crucified with Christ on the cross but that Jesus paid the price for our sins for all of mankind. The crucifixion gives us the opportunity to fellowship with Him for eternity. We share in the burden of carrying the cross and are to seek God's will for us at all cost.

Galatians 2:20 NIV

I have been crucified with Christ and I no longer live, but Christ lives in me. The life I now live in the body, I live by faith in the Son of God, who loved me and gave himself for me.

2 Timothy 1:7 NIV

For the Spirit God gave us does not make us timid, but gives us power, love and self-discipline.

Lastly, we are to follow Christ in our surrender. Jesus invited Andrew and Peter to follow him and they left everything behind to do so. It is tough to follow because we like being in the lead. We are impatient and want to move ahead at our own speed. We often feel that God is moving to slowly thus reviving the tug of war for control of the throne again. When we proceed on our own, we leave the safety of His will for the uncertainty of our own.

Being a dedicated follower of Christ requires wisdom and strength but most assuredly the ability to surrender control and exist within the parameters of God's will for us.

Find your life. Simply put, anyone seeking to save their own life by chasing their own interests and rejecting God's free gift of Jesus Christ, will inherit instead a shallow, meaningless life away from Him for eternity. Those who reject Him, have no hope or place in Heaven.

To surrender to Jesus God's Son is the most important decision a person can make. May God bless you with the perfect choice.

Proverbs 23:36 NIV

Do not let your heart envy sinners, but always be zealous for the fear of the LORD. There is surely a future hope for you, and your hope will not be cut off. Listen, my son, and be wise, and keep your heart on the right path.

Resilience

The recent pandemic crisis was cause for a long lockdown. I do not respond well to orders, so I did as I pleased. I only isolated when I actually got the Covid virus. I have an immune system disorder and several other co-morbid disease processes happening. I was cautioned that I would not have a good outcome if I contracted Covid. I was sick for sure but have had the flu in the past that was far more severe and felt like I was going to die, clingy tightly to life but wanting death to end my suffering. I was actually extremely close to it. The only explanation for why I didn't die is, I'm resilient. Also, God wasn't ready for me to die yet.

I'm so resilient that I've lived long past predictions of my demise living with a multitude of serious and terminal health issues. I have even been advised to make my final plans. I did and I'm still present and accounted for. This is comforting evidence that "God" is in control and nothing happens without His say so. It doesn't matter what illnesses I have, I refuse to live like I'm dying. I live as if I'm alive because I am.

Grace and resiliency are a process and outcome of successfully adapting to difficult or challenging life experiences. These challenges can include trauma or abuse, violence, neglect or serious health circumstances.

Perseverance is a common theme in God's Word. It's also referred to as endurance, patience, and long suffering. God grows the personal qualities in us through the process of sanctification. Hebrews points to the example of Jesus as our model of perseverance.

Hebrews 12:1-3 NIV

Therefore, since we are surrounded by such a great cloud of witnesses, let us throw off everything that hinders and the sin that so easily entangles. And let us run with perseverance the race marked out for us, fixing our eyes on Jesus, the pioneer and perfecter of faith.

One can grow stronger through mental and emotional trials utilizing flexibility in response to external and internal demands and practicing deep breathing. Use it often. It is not a cure for all our emotional issues but a help in giving over our cares and suffering to God. God encourages us to cast our cares at His feet and lay our burdens down.

Becoming resilient is possible along with finding contentment in the face of trauma. Change your narrative and become your best advocate adapting to difficult, stressful and adverse situations in life by accepting the healing God desires for us. Not that our past will change or go away but that God will handle the sting.

1 Corinthians 9:24 ESV

Do you not know that in a race all the runners run, but only one receives the prize? So run that you may obtain it.

Experiencing anger, misfortune and trauma can also grow you stronger through resilience. One can experience all the emotions from trials and tribulations and still become resilient and have contentment and happiness in life.

Becoming resilient in the face of abuse or trauma, does not take away the assault to one's body, mind and spirit. Nothing is erased just processed differently. God can help you to grow into resiliency with His grace and mercy.

Through Christ's love, our circumstances in life, devastating or wonderful are known to God. His love is stronger than any evil we may have encountered in this oft times unpleasant and unfortunate life.

Isaiah 58:8 NIV

Then your light will break forth like the dawn, and your healing will quickly appear; then your righteousness will go before you, and the glory of the LORD will be your rear guard.

Psalm 147:3 NIV

He heals the brokenhearted
And binds up their wounds.

Proverbs 3:8 ESV

It will be healing to your body
And refreshment to your bones.

Isaiah 57:18 KJV

I have seen his ways, and will heal him: I will lead him also, and restore comforts unto him and to his mourners.

Evil prevails in this world. The world contains sinful beings. However it is God who decides what happens on earth. Though evil runs rampant, spreading deceit and doing murderous things, Jesus has authority over all things and Heaven. Even though Satan is a roaring lion, we do not need to walk in fear but stay in God's light. Resist Satan and stand firm in your faith securely in God's love.

In an effort to love others harder, keeping them in prayer and seeking others to keep them in prayer is important.

Daniel 4:17 ESV

The sentence is by the decree of the watchers, the decision by the word of the holy ones, to the end that the living may know that the Most High rules the kingdom of men and gives it to whom he will and "sets over it the lowliest of men.'

Psalm 33:10-11 NIV

Hear, Lord, and be merciful to me; Lord, be my help."

You turned my wailing into dancing; you removed my sackcloth and clothed me with joy, The Lord brings the counsel of the nations to nothing; he frustrates the plans.

Mark 1:27 KJV

And they were all amazed, insomuch that they questioned among themselves, saying, What thing is this? what new doctrine is this? for with authority commandeth he even the unclean spirits, and they do obey him.

Deuteronomy 32:39

"See now that I, even I, am he, and there is no god beside me; I kill and I make alive; I wound, and I heal. Neither is there any That can deliver out of my hand.

HOW TO LOVE THE DIFFICULT

I've collected more difficult people in my lifetime than adults who know how to properly communicate. During the Covid lockdown I used the quite time alone to make some significant changes in my life. The first change was to eliminate all the horribly dysfunctional and toxic relationships that plagued me.

It was scary to think about it let alone make it happen. I was very successful in doing it accept for one relationship. What I have managed is to limit my contact with that person and not put up with their constant criticism of me.

It is hard work to reprogram all your trauma responses. They occur as if on auto pilot. I'm aware of them but have to have constant pep talks with my inner child in order to assure her.

To be a loving servant of Christ, it is important to have a clear understanding of how much you are loved and cherished by God. Though we are incomplete in many ways, God loves us completely. Even in our imperfect state of messiness, we are loved in the most perfect way. When we are lost and adrift without a compass, God's love encompasses us completely.

There is nowhere we can hide and there is nothing He doesn't see. We are an open book. God knows us better than we know or understand ourselves. God loves us because He is filled with an infinite measure of indescribable, holy, pure and perfect love for us.

Godly rules of life

1. Ask God into the pain of your past. He was with you always and understands.
2. What God thinks of you is a priority.
3. Time heals nothing but God heals completely.
4. God is always in charge.
5. God has His hand on everyone.
6. Stop worrying because God's got this!
7. Smile. You are loved more than you can imagine by God. That is worth a grin.

Always remember when you are in the process of loving harder that we are all created in the image of God. See Him even in your enemies face. Pray harder to begin to love harder.

Ever wonder why some people seem unlovable, including yourself from time to time? Are there seemingly " impossible to love" people in your life at this time. Maybe they are a complete mess from controlling, annoying, mean or they just don't like other people in general.

Suppose you consider what could have happened in someone's past to make them seemingly unlovable. But the reality is it's easiest to love people who are most like us or love us back. What really makes someone lovable is that they are loved. That you made the decision to love them, which has nothing to do with who you love but has everything to do with your capacity to love others.

Each of us is blessed with different gifts and different capacities. These are closely tied into our experiences which affects our ability and capacity to love. Our personal lives affects how we view others, even God.

We've all had opportunities to love those who are more difficult, needy and messy. As a rule, we tend to overlook those people and often neglect to pray for them.

Matthew 5:10-12 ESV

"Blessed are those who are persecuted for righteousness' sake, for utheirs is the kingdom of heaven. "Blessed are you when others revile you and persecute you and utter all kinds of evil against you falsely hon my account. Rejoice and be glad, for your reward is great in heaven, for jso they persecuted the prophets who were before you.

Matthew 7:12 NIV

So in everything, do to others what you would have them do to you, for this sums up the Law and the Prophets.

Galatians 5:14-15 NIV

For the entire law is fulfilled in keeping this one command: "Love your neighbor as yourself." If you bite and devour each other, watch out or you will be destroyed by each other.

Oddly enough, we have people around us who think we are difficult to love. This is sometimes evidenced through the family silent treatment.

We all have opportunities to love people we encounter who are just difficult. In my own family, it has been decided by most that they don't like me and are not speaking to me and are fine if they never do.

There are many reasons for this, but the overriding excuse is that I work hard on myself to untangle the proverbial barbwire ball. No one else in the family does that. They are all self medicating too. Where that leaves me is "the designated patient:" As the identifiable patient, they are the one family member in the dysfunctional family who expresses the families authentic inner conflicts.

This is an unenviable position to be in because essentially I'm the trouble maker and family "problem." I used to be hurt by the alienation when first diving into wellness but it does not impact my life any longer. I'm not responsible for them, they are adults and can make choices as they see fit.

I have a surrogate family that God provided me at age twelve. They were handpicked by Him and have loved me for 57 years. Families don't have to be blood relatives. They simply have to be the people who have chosen to love you, support you and welcome you into their family. It has been an amazing blessing to have this family present for me and loving me in spite of who I am, my sins, my past and my continuing sinful self.

I love my biological family also, so they have become my daily prayer project. This is how I love them honorably. They are also people I have to carry the cross of forgiveness for. It often requires I daily lift up the cross and offer them up to God's mercy and grace. A worthy cause I cannot manage without Christ's help. The more I pray for others, especially the difficult ones, the more my heart is softened towards them.

Ezekiel 36:26 NLT

And I will give you a new heart, and I will put a new spirit in you. I will take out your stony, stubborn heart and give you a tender, responsive heart.

Even the realization that their behavior is hateful, I don't think returning hate for hate is the answer. Yes, it spreads hate, but the bigger reason for me is selfish. When I respond with hatred, it affects how I feel about myself which is not good.

Focusing on negative things about someone else creates conflict within myself. I become uncomfortable and end up feeling conflicted and convicted. I can choose my responses and not visit those emotions.

I can choose to love people harder which creates good feelings in me. I'd rather choose to love than allow negative emotions create a defensive, offensive or judgmental attitude. When I choose to react negatively, I loose the power and control. My emotions are dictating my mood. I'd rather turn those people back over to God and stop the argument with God.

Unconditional love is a choice. It is a decision I make for my well being. Sometimes we have to actively make that decision over and over. It is our sin nature that creates the difficulty of staying on task. Changing our thought process also alters our life.

In choosing to love harder I keep my power and do not allow difficult or destructive people to sabotage my efforts. My need to respond to someone's backhanded comments or genuine dislike of me is really not my business. It just becomes a distraction of the enemy. I don't relish deliberately handling over my power to him willingly. I manage sin quite well without any help from outside sources.

LOVE INGENUITY

There is none other than or greater than, or possesses more ingenuity than God. Ingenuity requires immense skill and cleverness. God is the ultimate inventor.

Ingenuity - the desire and willingness to move when I need to move, and a willingness to be spontaneous and function without a script.

I've been blessed with a certain ingenuity and creativity which I'm grateful to God for. I can utilize my imaginary and creative side to develop new approaches to problems that might otherwise paralyze a lot of people. I embrace change, new ideas and desire growth in my life.

For me this means I may have to change gears quickly and accept many things on faith alone. We don't always know God's plans but can learn to trust that God is in charge. Sometimes this is painful. It seems scary to me because I'm often stuck in a particular way but also appreciate spontaneity.

I've spent years on the receiving end of plans gone awry. I don't want more pain and I don't need to know about more unknown painful things. I've had to switch gears the last few years to get where I am now. I needed to put old things in new places, thus changing my narrative for a different outcome.

Love - love yourself first in order to love others. We actually already do love ourselves first. Accept your flaws and shortcomings. Appreciate your gifts and talents and your fundamental human dignity. See others through the same lens with nothing else but the same human dignity. Choosing to love over other emotions frees me from the burden and fallout associated with those other emotions, especially negative ones.

I'm working harder at loving those harder, that I've been cheating and loving less.. It can be challenging as anything new can be. At first my response to loving harder was "why." People don't know how much or how little I'm loving them. It was quickly brought to my attention that people do pick up on how you feel about them. This is not an area you can fake people out on. They know. Paul spoke:

1 Corinthians 2:2 NIV

For I resolved to know nothing while I was with you except Jesus Christ and him crucified.

Paul is talking about Christ only in His ministry. Lest you forget, we're always supposed to be loving one another, harder. We have many reasons why we don't do it but no legitimate excuses.

Proverbs 22:29 NIV

Do you see someone skilled in their work? They will serve before kings; they will not serve before officials of low rank.

God's love is ingenious and evidence of His existence is all around us. God's wisdom and marvelous mysteries are everywhere too. The more aware we become of His constant thumbprint on everything, the more comforting His presence and majesty becomes.

Still, there are many people who will deny Him and His ownership of them. They are lost and don't understand who they are or who God is. Their existence and purpose are known to Him alone. God being everything good is also capable of wrath. Respect every aspect of who God is and cling to Him daily.

Romans 1:18-19 NKJV

For the wrath of God is revealed from heaven against all ungodliness and unrighteousness of men, who suppress the truth in unrighteousness, because what may be known of God is manifest in them, for dGod has shown it to them.

UNDERSTAND YOURSELF

It has been said that knowing who you are is great wisdom that humans possess. Learning who you are in relation to others helps you to understand and show up to love others as God calls us to do. Becoming self-aware helps us to navigate tricky emotional interactions and create safe boundaries with others. The ability to know yourself helps you to make more effective decisions and achieve desired goals.

We become empowered in managing ourselves effectively while helping build solid meaningful relationships with people we encounter on our journey.

So, who are you? Are you good at being self aware and actively working at being a better human? Changing who you are is an intense process of self-reflection and awareness of your behaviors and attitudes. It is learning to understand and process what motivates you and what triggers you. It's helpful to identify your strengths and weaknesses.

Doing so provides opportunities to explore what brings you happiness and what weighs you down.

I have always written down my thoughts, good and bad. It has been a substantial and therapeutic way for me to get out my emotions. It's a necessary tool in my life. It is where I draw my strength from. Writing frees my soul and gives wings to my thoughts and place in the world.

Writing also frees my heart much like my other artistic and creative endeavors. My baggage would weigh down my soul without the voice I summon in my writings.

When we gain clarity regarding our own heart through God's Word, we are able to see others more clearly. The more we understand ourselves and our neighbors, the more compassion, empathy and love we will have for them. These are vital emotions on our journey to love others harder.

Romans 13:8 USCCB

Owe nothing to anyone, except to love one another; for the one who loves another has fulfilled the law.

Love fulfills the law! God wants us to experience life-changing mercy, compassion and love. He wants us to receive this from Him and from those around us. In doing so we are able to give this love back to those we encounter as we sojourn through life.

Deuteronomy 15:7-8 NIV

If anyone is poor among your fellow Israelites in any of the towns of the land the LORD your God is giving you, do not be hardhearted or tightfisted toward them. Rather, be open handed and freely lend them whatever they need.

Job 6:14 ESV

"He who withholds kindness from a friend forsakes the fear of the Almighty."

The Bible tells us of Moses and how he chose to live his God-given identity. Moses was the greatest leader of the Old Testament. He understood himself and his destiny or "job" before him. Leading the

Jews to freedom after being enslaved for 400 years with the remaining 4th generation.

Hebrews 11:24-27 KJV

By faith Moses, when he was come to years, refused to be called the son of Pharaoh's daughter; Choosing rather to suffer affliction with the people of God, than to enjoy the pleasures of sin for a season;

Esteeming the reproach of Christ greater riches than the treasures in Egypt: for he had respect unto the recompence of the reward. By faith he forsook Egypt, not fearing the wrath of the king: for he endured, as seeing him who is invisible. By faith, Moses, when he had grown up, refused to be known as the son of Pharaoh's daughter. He chose to be mistreated along with the people of God rather than enjoy the fleeting pleasures of sin. He regarded disgrace for the sake of Christ as of greater value than the treasures of Egypt, because he was looking ahead to his reward. By faith he left Egypt, not fearing the king's anger; he persevered because he saw him who is invisible.

John 1:11-13 NIV

He came to that which was his own, but his own did not receive him. Yet to all who did receive him, to those who believed in his name, he gave the right to become children of God— children born not of natural descent, nor of human decision or a husband's will, but born of God.

John 1:10-13. NIV

He was in the world, and though the world was made through him, the world did not recognize him. He came to that which was his own, but his own did not receive him. Yet to all who did receive him, to those who believed in his name, he gave the right to become children of God— children born not of natural descent, nor of human decision or a husband's will, but born of God.

1 Corinthians 12:26-27 NIV

If one part suffers, every part suffers with it; if one part is honored, every part rejoices with it. Now you are the body of Christ, and each one of you is a part of it.

Understanding our identity and who we belong too creates a certainty and security in our destiny and ultimate destination. We do not have to search out an identity as we have been loved into existence.

True love directly from our Heavenly Father, grants us the capability and capacity to love others. When we know who and where we belong our sense of safety and assuredness settles into our bones and becomes part of how we interact with others. Love breeds love.

We are free to love as we are loved and taught love through God's holy Word. Ways we can love others are to be approachable and available. Be full of God's good Grace. Be bold and unafraid to speak God's truth. Be generous of self, offering your gifts and talents and prayers on your journey through life.

We are able to accomplish these things and do them with generosity of Spirit because we are assured who created us, loves us and frees us in the most amazing and generous way. Unconditionally!

We are called to be servants of Christ. Jesus helped people in all different circumstances. It did not matter who they were, Gentile or Jew. Reading through the gospels in the New Testament, we can read of Jesus showing and teaching us how to be a servant. Jesus put the needs of others before his own. He helped people to grow their faith and how to be kind and merciful to others.

There are some specific ways we can serve one another. These may change due to time, place and need. Things that servants have in common with one another are;

*Humility
*Readiness
*Perseverance

A servant is also prepared to serve where they are needed as directed by God. Additionally, a servant can expect to suffer. Christ was the ultimate suffering servant, taking sin and death upon himself on the cross.

Hebrews 12:10 NIV

They disciplined us for a little while as they thought best; but God disciplines us for our good, in order that we may share in his holiness.

2 Corinthians 4:17-18 KJV

For our light affliction, which is but for a moment, worketh for us a far more exceeding and eternal weight of glory;

While we look not at the things which are seen, but at the things which are not seen: for the things which are seen are temporal; but the things which are not seen are eternal.

Philippians 1:14 KJV

And most of the brothers, having become confident in the Lord by my imprisonment, are much more bold to speak the word without fear.

2 Corinthians 1:5-6 NIV

For just as we share abundantly in the sufferings of Christ, so also our comfort abounds through Christ. If we are distressed, it is for your comfort and salvation; if we are comforted, it is for your comfort, which produces in you patient endurance of the same sufferings we suffer.

1 Peter 4:16 ESV

Yet if anyone suffers as a Christian, let him not be ashamed, but let him glorify God in that name.

I have learned very late in life that my suffering has been ultimately beneficial. It grew me into someone who understands other people's suffering journey. I get it. Many people don't. I would not want to relive my traumatic years but I'm glad for them. Not much shakes up my world anymore because I've been there, done that already.

James 1:2-4 ESV

Count it all joy, my brothers, when you meet trials of various kinds, for you know that the testing of your faith produces steadfastness. And let steadfastness have its full effect, that you may be perfect and complete, lacking in nothing.

2 Corinthians 12:10 ESV

For the sake of Christ, then, I am content with weaknesses, insults, hardships, persecutions, and calamities. For when I am weak, then I am strong.

Philippians 3:7-8 NIV

But whatever were gains to me I now consider loss for the sake of Christ. What is more, I consider everything a loss because of the surpassing worth of knowing Christ Jesus my Lord, for whose sake I have lost all things. I consider them garbage, that I may gain Christ

Open your heart to be a willing and suffering servant of Christ! Understand the prophecy of the Atonement of Jesus Christ. Isaiah taught that the Savior would be despised and rejected, smitten and afflicted; that He would assume our sorrows and that He would be wounded for our transgressions. What a powerful and wonderful statement of who God is.

Isaiah 53:3-4 KJV

He is despised and rejected of men; a man of sorrows, and acquainted with grief: and we hid as it were our faces from him; he was despised, and we esteemed him not. Surely he hath borne our griefs, and carried our sorrows: yet we did esteem him stricken, smitten of God, and afflicted.

This is just one more reminder of what Jesus did for us on the cross. It provides us additional detail of His suffering and sacrifice. What a priceless gift to the people He loves. This was an amazing gift that we did absolutely nothing to receive.

LOVE AT WORK

G od is the blueprint for love. We are unable, uncoordinated and impossibly dumb when it comes to effective love strategies. We desperately need a Savior. We can be wholly inadequate like clowns in a circus when it comes to loving people harder.

We can be acrobatically amusing for the entertainment and pleasure of others. Able to teeter gracefully and endure endless pratfalls and pies in the face. However, not taken seriously. As clowns, people are expected to laugh uproariously at the ensuing sideshow we refer to as life. We do not want to leave people cringing in fear and horror as sometimes happens. We need to rise above our difficult circumstances with God's help.

Without the blueprint we are just circus clowns, unable to manage on our own. We've often proven our inability to make the best choices and carry them out without incident or negative consequences.it cannot be emphasized enough the need for Christ's direction.

It is easier to spot love gone wrong than it is love gone right. More attention is paid to relationships that are struggling or failing. How do we manage to frequently make a mess out of love? What does true love even look like?

True love can be achieved by working at it and with the proper tools. It must incorporate admiration, respect and care along with humility. There should be no emotional pain inflicted or any form of abuse towards another person.

Genuine love is sought after and/or desired and yet can be quite elusive. People often assume they are in love but are confusing it with infatuation. Love is also pure happiness, filling your days with joy. It allows for generous respect and healthy give and take.

Genuine love is respectful and goes to great lengths to improve upon and work at keeping others happy. This love is not a 50/50 contract but is a 100%/100% commitment to the wellbeing of a relationship and nurtures the relationship with a sense of pride.

It takes work to maintain a wonderful loving relationship with another person. We all have particular feelings, needs and desires. Part of a maturing love relationship is a lack of jealousy along with realistic expectations and demonstrations of love.

Love isn't confined to romantic relationships. There is deep love in families and amongst friends. This love follows the same basic guidelines but without physical contact or romantic love.

People also fall in love with their pets and their things. But what true love actually "feels" like in a more defined way, is like the combined best parts from any great relationship. When you are truly in love, it feels like the best friendship you've ever had including the additional bonus of an ongoing physical attraction and intimacy.

Love builds on itself. It grows like a flower. You know your love is meaningful when the thought of losing your love physically hurts. Also when you are able to feel pain for the person you love.

God teaches us love through His Word and through the people He carefully places on your path. People who love you, show up for a reason. God does not plan accidents or coincidences. God deliberately created the whole earth and then He created you, for the sole purpose of being loved by Him.

1 John 4:18 NIV

Without this blueprint we are like circus clowns, unable to manage on our own. We've repeatedly proved our inability to make the best choices and carry them out without love.

God's love is infinite, personal and unconditional. That is love with power behind it. It's a mighty force unto itself. We get a glimpse of that love in our lifetime but will not understand it's true power until we meet God in Heaven.

Romans 8:35-37 KJV

Who shall separate us from the love of Christ? shall tribulation, or distress, or persecution, or famine, or nakedness, or peril, or sword? As it is written, For thy sake we are killed all the day long; we are accounted as sheep for the slaughter. Nay, in all these things we are more than conquerors through him that loved usho shall separate us from the love of Christ?

God commands us to love and follow Him as well as love one another. The enemy works hard to drive wedges between people, especially Christians in the church. The enemy's greatest victory is to cause discord and division within the church walls.

God is more powerful than anything on earth or in Heaven. Accept God's invitation to enter into a relationship with Him and know His immense love that you can be forever secure in.

God will never abandon you. Even when things get difficult and seem impossible to unravel, God is with us. God knows everything we've done wrong and what we will do, and yet we are still loved. God's truth is He will never stop loving us.

Grace Triumphant

The word grace originally meant " God's favor or help." This is a sense of how we still use it today. The related word "gracious" originally meant "filled with God's favor or help." The Latin translation "gratia" meant a pleasing quality, thanks or favor, from gratus meaning, "pleasing."

Grace is the power that God gives to us willingly in order for us to do what we cannot do on our own without His Divine intervention on our behalf. God spoke to Paul "my grace is sufficient for you" supplying Paul with the power to be freed from the thorn in his flesh.

2 Corinthians 12:7 NIV

Or because of these surpassingly great revelations. Therefore, in order to keep me from becoming conceited, I was given a thorn in my flesh, a messenger of Satan, to torment me.

Grace brings to us new life which God does not condemn. Through God's grace our way of thinking is transformed and renewed. We are forgiven and our mind and heart changed. Through grace we live life as God wants each of His children to experience. We gain freedom in living in Christ.

As a divinely offered gift, God's grace, does not restrict or detract from our individual freedom. It perfects our freedom by restricting and aiding us to overcome the true obstacle of our freedom which is the power sin has in our lives. The grace of the Holy Spirit, received by faith in Jesus Christ is the New Law.

God willingly gives us the help we need to do what we are unable to do under our own power. When practicing grace, we are choosing to interact in a sinful world with courtesy and good will towards others. This doesn't mean it's alright to disregard boundaries but allows you the space to be flexible with kindness, acceptance and perseverance.

It is God who produces grace and enhances and develops salvation. God's grace alone has the potential for changing someone's life in a powerful way. Grace is not the only amazing experience we are to have with God.

Romans 3:24 NLT

Yet God, in his grace, freely makes us right in his sight. He did this through Christ Jesus when he freed us from the penalty for our sins.

Grace is what inclines God to provide gifts that are free and undeserved by all sinners. This spontaneous, unmerited gift of Divine favor for the salvation of sinners is God's influence operating in us for our regeneration and sanctification.

Grace is an acronym representing five different attributes:

G-generosity
R-respect
A-action
C-compassion
E-energy

We benefit from grace as the Lord's grace is sufficient to do what we cannot normally do if left to our own devices. Grace is giving people more than they deserve.

If we choose to live simply and not allow our daily schedules or other people, including our possessions to suffocate us, our attention can be focused on what we find beautiful, useful or meaningful in life. If you let the rest go, it is possible to create a sanctuary in our home and in our hearts. Spend as much time as possible in nature. God can more readily be felt and visualized in the outdoors.

God's grace as a gift divinely offered does not take away from our freedom but rather perfects in us our freedom by helping us to restrict and overcome the power that sin has in our lives. Sin being our one true obstacle to our individual freedom becoming slaves to it.

HOW TO SHOW GRACE TO ONE ANOTHER;

1. Words. Be kind and gentle in what you say and how you say it.
2. Look for Needs and Opportunities. Simple everyday kindnesses and actions often help in great ways.
3. Let it Go.
4. Be There.
5. Forgive.
6. Learn to Ask for Forgiveness.
7. Watch the Way You Speak. 8. Have Gratitude.

Jesus does not discriminate against His people because God's grace has sufficient coverage for everyone. It doesn't matter how deep or far away your sin has taken you, Jesus' forgiveness is always assured.

How do we as sinners access God's grace? In order to flow in God's good grace you need a strong habit of prayer and returning to God's throne of grace at all times. If you are lacking help you are likely lacking grace. A constant flow of grace enables you to find help when it is needed. God's spirit of grace is in the spirit of prayer. Pray unceasingly.

How do we access God's grace? We can do so by believing what God's Word has to say about His people and allowing that to guide and protect you. Embracing God's truth and rebuking lies, thus living life by God's faith, provided to us.

When we model faith to others, it is showing kindness to someone else when they don't even deserve it. Much how God treats us.

Granting grace is going beyond compassion and kindness. It is loving someone even though they might not deserve it or ever reciprocate that love. God's grace is available and waiting for every broken spirit. Be repentant.

Romans 6:1 NIV

What shall we say, then? Shall we go on sinning so that grace may increase?

God's Word tells us that we are saved by grace through faith in Christ Jesus and not by our own efforts or works. God's grace is available to everyone who is willing to humble themselves and accept Jesus as their Lord and Savior in order to receive forgiveness. Forgiveness is available to us daily for those willing to humble themselves and seek God for help along with the ability to come against sin that continues to rise up in each of us.

Grace gives us the genuine and generous desire to do good in His name. Jesus pours out His grace granting us the power to choose doing good and with that choose freedom fulfilling our journey as children of God.

Ephesians 2:8-9 NIV

For it is by grace you have been saved, through faith—and this is not from yourselves, it is the gift of God—not by works, so that no one can boast.

GOD AND EMPATHY

The New Testament testifies that God is an empathetic God and that His empathy extends beyond our capacity to rationalize the human experience. God actively enters into the human experience as our guide and help.

There are three different kinds of empathy being Cognitive, Emotional and Compassionate. Empathy can be as simple as just smiling at someone. Giving someone your full attention is also empathy. Those who do not have any empathy are considered psychopaths.

The gift of empathy is about reflecting God's compassion, not magnifying the gloom or hopelessness that someone has.

Psalm 86:15 KJV

But thou, O Lord, art a God full of compassion, and gracious, long suffering, and plenteous in mercy and truth.

Nehemiah 9:7 NIV

You are the Lord God, who chose Abram and brought him out of Ur of the Chaldeans and named him Abraham.

Empathy is woven deep into the fabric of Scripture. Every instruction of God offers the way we are to treat others with empathy.

1 Peter 3:8 NIV

Finally, all of you, be like-minded, be sympathetic, love one another, be compassionate and humble.

What Peter refers to is the mind of Christ. Peters' call for unity cannot be answered without empathy and understanding. In order to be one with another person we need to have a good understanding of:

*who they are
*how they became that person
*what they know
*how they learned it
* what they hold dear
*why they hold it dear
*how they feel
*why they feel that way

When it's important to show empathy it can be done in simple ways such as, listening with the goal to understanding. Generally what people need is just to feel heard by someone. Ask questions with genuine curiosity and be fully present. Don't let your biases become part of the conversation and don't offer unsolicited advice. It's important to make eye contact, acknowledge one's feelings and relay similar experiences if you have them.

According to Peter, oneness is created by treating each other with compassion, love, tenderness and courtesy. Four qualities that lie at the heart of empathy.

Romans 12:15 KJV

Rejoice with them that do rejoice, and weep with them that weep.

The urge to send our thoughts and prayers from a distance is hard to resist, but that is not what empathy is and that is not what God calls us to do. We are to be active with empathy not passive.

John 15:35 KJV

The man departed, and told the Jews that it was Jesus, which had made him whole.

Hebrews 4:15 ESV

For we do not have a high priest who is unable to sympathize with our weaknesses, but one who in every respect has been tempted as we are, yet without.

What makes Jesus an especially effective counselor and defender is his time on earth. He expertly represents us before God, because He empathizes with us.

Psalm 84:11 AMP

For the LORD God is a sun and shield; The LORD bestows grace and favor and honor; No good thing will He withhold from those who walk uprightly.

We grapple with what it means to love our neighbor and live out our faith in our community. Christ understands us because He endured what we've endured. Understanding is key.

Diving into the mess instead of avoiding the mess is God's method of caring and empathy. Instead of passively offering prayer. Prayer is of utmost importance but so often faith in action is required to really be present for others.

John 13:34 NIV

"A new command I give you: Love one another. As I have loved you, so you must love one another."

Heed the great calling and offer empathy as God has granted us His. It can be a blessing and healing gift for others.

OUR STORMS

L ife is full of storms to be sure. Getting through them requires maturity, patience, support and God. Storms come with the possibility of death and destruction. Learning ways to navigate storms is crucial to survival. God is our ever present help during the storms of life.

Storms in scripture often represent God's power and amazing presence. When we encounter personal tragedies in life we respond with similar feelings as God does, such as darkness, lightning, earthquakes and fire. These are ways God manifests His greatness.

Isaiah 25:4 NIV

You have been a refuge for the poor, a refuge for the needy in their distress, a shelter from the storm and a shade from the heat. For the breath of the ruthless is like a storm driving against a wall.

We all experience storms in life. It is in these turbulent times that we wonder and ask, where is God? Why is this happening? Did I do something wrong? Did God make this happen? We actually have the answers in God's Word.

These are some possible reasons:

GOD MAY BE SEEKING OUR ATTENTION.

The Lord speaks gently to our hearts but sometimes He has to increase the volume to be heard. He does this out of love to protect us from our sin.

Romans 15:4 NIV
For everything that was written in the past was written to teach us, so that through the endurance taught in the Scriptures and the encouragement they provide we might have hope.

GOD MAY BE CALLING US TO REPENT.

God used a literal storm to get Jonah's attention. We cannot ever avoid God because He is present everywhere.

Jonah 11:2-3 KJV
(It was that Mary which anointed the Lord with ointment, and wiped his feet with her hair, whose brother Lazarus was sick.) Therefore his sisters sent unto him, saying, Lord, behold, he whom thou lovest is sick.

GOD WANTS US TO CONFORM TO CHRISTS IMAGE.

God is willing to break us in order to glorify Himself to make us more like His Son.

1 Peter 4:13 KJV
but rejoice, inasmuch as ye are partakers of Christ's sufferings; that, when his glory shall be revealed, ye may be glad also with exceeding joy.

God who is faithful and just will always be there when we seek Him through storms and when we go astray. He has as many reasons to do so as there are sinners who need His guidance and protection.

Isaiah 54:11 KJV

O thou afflicted, tossed with tempest, and not comforted, behold, I will lay thy stones with fair colours, and lay thy foundations with sapphires.

In order to face life's storms we should always remember God's promises to us. Stay in conversation with God and believe in His love for us. Be patient and rely on the faith God has granted each of us to weather storms.

Philippians 4:19 NIV

And my God will meet all your needs according to the riches of his glory in Christ Jesus.

God is always with us in every storm. He never abandons us to our sin and wandering. We can be assured and reassured in His glorious words to us.

2 Corinthians 12:9 KIV

But he said to me, "My grace is sufficient for you, for my power is made perfect in weakness." Therefore I will boast all the more gladly about my weaknesses, so that Christ's power may rest on me.

DISCERNING JUDGMENT

T he Bible speaks to us regarding judgment and there are different kinds of judgment referenced in God's Word. It's important to understand their differences so that we do not miss the mark and are making proper use of the them.

Judgment is discernment. It is taking notice of behavior that is not scriptural, moral or legal and speaking openly to it. We have a responsibility to help address sin operating in someone's life.

The scriptures tell about past judgments such as Adam and Eve banished from the garden and the all encompassing flood. Also included is the story of the Tower of Babel and the judgment against Egypt. Lastly, there is the judgment of believers. Jesus took this judgment upon Himself by His crucifixion and death. Our sin was "judgment" at the cross, Jesus died for us to save us from the judgment of our sin.

Romans 8:1 NKJV

There is therefore now no condemnation to those who are in Christ Jesus, who do not walk according to the flesh, but according to the Spirit.

There are current judgements happening in the church. They are self evaluation and divine discipline. The church aids in this process to purify the body of Christ. Self judgment requires spiritual discernment, with the goal of being more Christ-like.

God's judgment is for instruction telling us about His character and person. God's judgment can often be difficult for us to understand. That happens because we do not always comprehend His ways.

Isaiah 55:9 NIV

"As the heavens are higher than the earth, so are my ways higher than your ways and my thoughts than your thoughts.

It is important to understand that God's understanding is higher than ours. Even though we can study God's Word in an effort to know everything about Him, it does not reveal every detail of His actions nor the reasons behind those actions.

1 Corinthians 11:28 NIV

Everyone ought to examine themselves before they eat of the bread and drink from the cup.

God also brings His followers to a place of self repentance and restoration when they sin. In doing so, God distinguishes between his flock and the rest of the world.

1 Corinthians 11:32 NLT

Yet when we are judged by the Lord, we are being disciplined so that we will not be condemned along with the world.

There are also judgments to come in the future. The judgements of the tribulation against the wicked, will leave no doubt of God's wrath against sin.

Revelations 6-16-17 KJV

And said to the mountains and rocks, Fall on us, and hide us from the face of him that sitteth on the throne, and from the wrath of the Lamb: For the great day of his wrath is come; and who shall be able to stand

Additionally, there is the judgment seat of Christ, where believers will be judged according to their faithfulness in Christian service. Their sins being bought and paid for on the cross. Selfish acts or those done without mercy will be burned up.

Corinthians 3:12-13 USCCB

If anyone builds on this foundation with gold, silver, precious stones, wood, hay, or straw, the work of each will come to light, for the Day* will disclose it. It will be revealed with fire, and the fire [itself] will test the quality of each one's work.

After the tribulation, Jesus will sit in judgment over the Gentile nations. They will be judged according to their treatment of Israel during the tribulation. This judgment is called the judgment of the goats and sheep.

Matthew 25:31-33 ESV

"When the Son of Man comes in his glory, and all the angels with him, then he will sit on his glorious throne. Before him will be gathered all the nations, and he will separate people one from another as a shepherd separates the sheep from the goats. And he will place the sheep on his right, but the goats on the left.

There is also the judgment of angels. Angels are not created in God's image and are not redeemed by Christ. As God's children, we will be given a higher position than angels. God also sends His angels to serve His saints, those individuals who will inherit eternal life.

Hebrews 1:14 NIV

Are not all angels ministering spirits sent to serve those who will inherit salvation.

We also know the Greek word for judge, krino, means "to rule or govern." This strongly suggests that we will have authority over the angels for they have no sin for which they can be "judged" in the sense of being "condemned." Likely the understanding of this is that believers will sit in judgment over fallen angels and rule over holy angels. Christ being exalted above all angels.

1 Corinthians 6:1-3 NIV

If any of you has a dispute with another, do you dare to take it before the ungodly for judgment instead of before the Lord's people? Or do you not know that the Lord's people will judge the world? And if you are to judge the world, are you not competent to judge trivial cases? If any of you have a dispute with another, do you dare to take it before the ungodly for judgment instead of before the Lord's people? Or do you not know the Lord's people will judge the world ? And if you are to judge the world, are you not competent to judge trivial cases?

We are called to use good judgment and discernment in the world. We are to understand the purpose and weight of addressing another's sin. We are not to judge others as the people whom they are, but recognize and judge the sin they may be involved in.

Matthew 7:1 NIV

"Do not judge, or you too will be judged

John 7:24 NKJV

Do not judge according to appearance, but judge with righteous judgment.

Psalm 119:68 NIV

You are good, and what you do is good; teach me your decrees.

1 Corinthians 6:2-3 ESV

Or do you not know that sthe saints will judge the world? And if the world is to be judged by you, are you incompetent to try trivial cases?

1 Kings 3:9 NIV

So give your servant a discerning heart to govern your people and to distinguish between right and wrong. For who is able to govern this great people of yours?"

Do not let people tell you as Christians we are not to "judge." That is not exactly accurate. We are not supposed to be blind or ignore sin within our Christian and church families and sin in the world.

We should pray first before confronting sin. It's always good to be kneeling when possible while praying. It reminds us who God is and who we are in relationship to Him.

The term "judgement" can spark ferocious debate. I've lost important friendships with people over biblical misunderstandings regarding judgment.

Non-Christians jump all over the word as a weapon to thrust into Christians regarding everything they fundamentally believe and may be misinformed about God's Word.

Judgment and discernment are necessary tools on our Christian walk. They keep us aware.

Jesus' Love

How much does Jesus love me? We all want to be in a relationship with someone who loves us very much. We also want the love that comes our way quantified. God's Word answers that question. Even though we are incomplete sinful beings, God loves us completely.

Our lives should be a reflection of God's love and also reflect a merciful relationship with Christ. If you are walking with Christ on the inside then your words, decisions and actions should show a distinctness of God on the outside too.

We will never be able to fully comprehend how much Jesus loves us. The human mind is not big enough to fully grasp the love of God. In Heaven perhaps we will finally know the extent of that love.

Here are some ways we can know God loves us:

God created you.

Psalm 139

He knew you before you were born.

Christ died for you.

Romans 5:8 KJV

But God commendeth his love toward us, in that, while we were yet sinners, Christ died for us.

He gave us the Bible.

John 10:10 KJV

The thief cometh not, but for to steal, and to kill, and to destroy: I am come that they might have life, and that they might have it more abundantly.

He keeps His word.

Genesis 46:27 ESV

And the sons of Joseph, who were born to him in Egypt, were two. All the persons of the house of Jacob who came into Egypt were seventy.

He has plans for you.

Proverbs 19:21 NIV

Many are the plans in a person's heart, but it is the LORD's purpose that prevails

God's purpose prevails.

He wants a relationship with you.

Matthew 6:33 USCCB

No one can serve two masters. He will either hate one and love the other, or be devoted to one and despise the other. You cannot serve God and mammon.

God's redeeming love frees us of guilt and fear. God loves us with justifying love. God justifies us by declaring us innocent. Christ is treated as if He were the sinner and the sinner is treated as if they were the righteous one. This is far more than what we deserve.

1 John 3:1 NIV

See what great love the Father has lavished on us, that we should be called children of God! And that is what we are! The the world does not know us is that it did not.

Romans 8:38-39 KJV

For I am persuaded, that neither death, nor life, nor angels, nor principalities, nor powers, nor things present, nor things to come. Nor height, nor depth, nor other creature, shall be able to separate us from the love of God, which is in Christ Jesus our Lord.

The cross is God's complete expression of sacrifice and love for us. His love is so important, pure and complete that it is all we need and more. Where else in the world can you find such perfect love?

Romans 5:8 NIV

But God demonstrates his own love for us in this: While we were still sinners, Christ died for us.

God sees each of us as an individual and collectively. In a personal relationship with Him or in relationship to one another. A relationship is where we learn about who God is along with God's Word.

God views us as His beloved children. He has authority, He leads and teaches; He loves His child, He guides, instructs and even disciplines His children when called for.

Our identity is as His children. Children blessed by Him. This helps us to safely trust God with our children as they are His beloved children too.

Isaiah 54:13 KJV

All your children shall be taught by the Lord,

Romans 8:14 NIV

In order that the righteous requirement of the law might be fully met in us, who do not live according to the flesh but according to the Spirit.

Galatians 3:26 NIV

So in Christ Jesus you are all children of God through faith.

He knows us intimately and loves us abundantly without reservation or hesitation. That is a love worth pursuing and love to be returned exponentially. Jesus modeled this love to His people. That was His mission everywhere He went. Jesus made those who were sick well again. He restored sight to a blind man. He also liberated those who were bound by social injustice and prejudice. He loved harder. Jesus had respect for everyone and showed it lovingly.

LIVING FORGIVEN

P **salm 139:23-24 NIV**

Search me, God, and know my heart; test me and know my anxious thoughts. See if there is any offensive way in me, and lead me in the way everlasting.

God hates sin but He loves us sinners. God's price for forgiveness is high, as He has paid that price himself. A tortuous death on the cross. That is loving harder.

Through Christ's loving act of grace, believers are eternally freed from the penalty of guilt and sin. Covered in Christ's blood, God no longer keeps a record of our sin. The forgiveness of God is totally complete.

Psalm 32:1-2 ESV

Blessed is the one whose transgression is forgiven,

whose sin is covered.

Blessed is the man against whom the Lord counts no iniquity, and in whose spirit there is no deceit.

Isaiah 43:25 NIV

I, even I, am he who blots out your transgressions, for my own sake, and remembers your sins no more.

As believers, we receive God's forgiveness when we repent of our sin and place our faith in Christ for salvation. Those sins, past, present and future, big or small, are forgiven forever. Still, when we stumble and we are called to confess our sins.

1 John 1:9 KJV

If we confess our sins, he is faithful and just to forgive us our sins, and to cleanse us from all unrighteousness

Yes, as Christians we sin, but we are not to be identified by a life of sin. As believers, we are a new creation in Christ. As Christians we should be living a changed life, growing more Christ-like as we mature.

Change does not happen instantly but over a lifetime. A person should grow from producing acts of the flesh to producing fruits of the Spirit.

1 Corinthians 6:11 NIV

And that is what some of you were. But you were washed, you were sanctified, you were justified in the name of the Lord Jesus Christ and by the Spirit of our God.

We have all sinned and deserve God's judgment. God the Father however, sent His only Son to satisfy that judgment for those who believe. Jesus the creator and eternal Son of God, who lived a sinless life, loved us so much, He took our sins with Him to the cross, receiving the punishment that we deserve.

Psalm 103:12 NIV

As far as the east is from the west, so far has he removed our transgressions from us.

It is possible for the Lord to look at us and not see our sins because He forgave us, He removed our sins from us and has granted us eternal life.

In our humanity exists our frailty along with our sin. We were created by God to lean on Him, through His Son Jesus Christ. His sacrificial death on the cross gave us forgiveness drawing us closer to our Heavenly Father. Through the Holy Spirit we are convicted as believers to confess and repent our sin.

1 Peter 3:18 USCCB

For Christ also suffered* for sins once, the righteous for the sake of the unrighteous, that he might lead you to God. Put to death in the flesh, he was brought to life in the spirit.

John 10:10 KJV

The thief cometh not, but for to steal, and to kill, and to destroy: I am come that they might have life, and that they might have it more abundantly.

Forgiveness is an act of obedience and gratefulness to God. It is letting go of our sin. Scripture tells us to forgive everyone, everything, every time. It is an acknowledgment of the sacrifice God made through His Son Jesus to restore the relationship between God and man. In doing so He took upon Himself the sins of the world.

Forgiveness can be hard, requiring us to understand why it matters. When we finally get why forgiveness is so important we then need to practice forgiveness becoming "forgiveness fit."

In the process we should address our own inner pain and become empathic to ourselves by understanding about our own suffering. When forgiveness is hard, call upon God and your own strengths. It may require you to pick up the cross of forgiveness on a daily basis to helping you to understand it's importance.

When we practice forgiveness of others, we are receiving Gods forgiveness for ourselves.

Blessed in the mess.

CHERISH ONE ANOTHER

It is so very important to cherish people in your life. To show genuine love and regard for one another is our greatest command from God after first loving Him. Those we cherish reap positive results based on your continuous efforts. Cherishing others brings about their happiness. It makes for a better world as happiness flows from those we cherish.

How is it that we allow insignificant differences in politics, relationships and life itself alter our ability to cherish someone. That we allow anger to fester into indifference and abandonment of people we love and care about. Going about our day oblivious to those we may have injured along the way, directly or out of ignorance. Seek deeper understanding and awareness of your feelings and emotions.

Ephesians 5:25 NIV
Husbands, love your wives, just as Christ loved the church and gave himself up for her.

Jesus calls us to love, over and over. There are well over a hundred scriptures in the Bible about the call to love one another.

Take a second look at your contribution to a breakdown in a relationship. Re-think love and extend it everywhere. It is more than likely that a lack of love is playing a role, especially in the church.

We are taught to cherish our family members but often leave out properly loving in our friendships and with total strangers. To openly love everyone plants a seed of happiness that has the opportunity to grow into a mighty forest as God nurtures the seed.

Love comes from God. We cannot manufacture it on our own. It is the same with faith.

As our love relationship grows with God, so our love grows to freely give as servants of God. Unable to create love on our own, we still have love to give in appreciation for others by keeping them special in our hearts.

1 John 4:7-8 NIV
Dear friends, let us love one another, for love comes from God. Everyone who loves has been born of God and knows God. Whoever does not love does not know God, because God is love.

1 John 4:17–19 ESV
By this ais love perfected with us, so that bwe may have confidence for the day of judgment, because cas he is so also are we in this world. 18 There is no fear in love, but perfect love casts out fear. For fear has to do with punishment, and whoever fears has not abeen perfected in love. We love because he first loved us and as we live in God, our love grows more perfect.

Psalm 66:18 NIV
If I had cherished sin in my heart, the Lord would not have listened.

John 16:33 ESV
I have said these things to you, that in me you may have peace. In the world you will have tribulation. But take heart; I have overcome the world.

To cherish all whom we encounter should become a discipline we wear as if it were a part of our bodies like a second skin.

It is not always easy to get along with everyone. Everyone you encounter becomes a part of your life and story. Regardless of mistakes and disagreements, they have held a place in your world. In some significant way we are all changed by our relationships with others.

Are you cherishing others or taking them for granted? Remember to cherish each person in your life. Create the time to really get to know them. Listen to their story. Understand their role in your life. Pay attention to what they have to teach you.

1 John 4:8 NIV

Whoever does not love does not know God, because God is love.

Romans 12:2 NIV

Do not conform to the pattern of this world, but be transformed by the renewing of your mind. Then you will be able to test and approve what God's will is—his good, pleasing and perfect will.

It can be hard to make the switch from anger, to cherishing and loving but it is the proffered walk with the Lord. Anger weighs down your heart in brokenness. It becomes more sin.

James 1:19-20 ESV

Let every person be quick to hear, slow to speak, slow to anger; for the anger of man does not produce the righteousness of God.

James 1:20 NIV

Because human anger does not produce the righteousness that God desires.

Because human anger does not produce the righteousness that God desires. Learn to stop and refocus when you're feeling angry and overwhelmed. This requires self awareness, patience and practice.

Cherish all and love one another as the Bible reminds us to do in Jesus' name. The act of cherishing others brings joy into their lives as well as yours.

CEASE STRIVING

P **salm 46:10 NIV**
He says, "Be still, and know that I am God; I will be exalted among the nations, I will be exalted in the earth.

God's exhortation to "cease striving" is a reassurance and invitation to serenely enjoy His fellowship and presence. All that is required is our faithful attendance. God in turn supplies everything else we need and helps to free us from the bondage of strife.

We can assume that this invitation comes along with a rebuke. In this scripture, God is rebuking the Hebrews for not trusting in Him. The Lord is responding as an angry parent trying to break up a fight between siblings. That while we attempt to defend ourselves, we often make matters worse.

1 Peter 5:7-9 NIV
Cast all your anxiety on him because he cares for you.

Be alert and of sober mind. Your enemy the devil prowls around like a roaring lion looking for someone to devour. Resist him, standing firm in the faith, because you know that the family of believers throughout the world is undergoing the same kind of sufferings.

In today's world, many have made "striving" into a virtue. We admire and reward overachievers for their sweat, hard work and diligence. It seems, the more a person pushes towards perfectionism, the more they are admired. We label that effort as a "good work ethic." But perfectionism becomes an idol that interferes with our relationship with God as serving two masters is not a viable option.

Luke 13:24 NIV
"Make every effort to enter through the narrow door, because many, I tell you, will try to enter and will not be able too.

"Striving" is devoting significant serious energy in an attempt to finish a project and/or win. It's a struggle in opposition. In the strife and struggle to land on top, we often forget to bring God into the picture. With God, strife and anxiety are not the goals for our lives. Peace and contentment are.

Ecclesiastes 1:14 NIV
I have seen all the things that are done under the sun; all of them are meaningless, chasing after the wind.

We need only to seek the God of the universe and lay our anxieties and burdens at the foot of the cross, to receive spiritual peace and rest in Him. Along with letting go, is the encouragement to ask God for His help and guidance in all things. We are called as His people to pray, petition and give thanks to the Lord in all things.

Philippians 4:6 KJV
Be careful for nothing; but in every thing by prayer and supplication with thanksgiving let your requests be made known unto God.

We are to stop trying to manufacture the outcome of our lives and the lives of others. It requires us to give up control. We are truly deficient in areas of control, when you consider the unsatisfactory final outcome we create.

Proverbs 3:5-6 KJV

Trust in the Lord with all thine heart; and lean not unto thine own understanding. In all thy ways acknowledge him, and he shall direct thy paths.

When we choose to lean on God, we give up our delusion of a stable, comfortable and upright position relying on ourselves. Leaning on God and letting go of our erroneous self reliable stance, begins trusting God with all our circumstances. Our faith then becomes active. God's work in us is the assurance we need on earth.

Psalm 146:3 KJV

Put not your trust in princes, nor in the son of man, In whom there is no help.

When we cease striving on our own, it becomes easier to surrender to God. It is letting God know we are not big enough to deal with our worries, and that He can take over. We give God permission to move with His might on our behalf as we get out of the way.

Resilience

G race and resiliency are a process and outcome of successfully adapting to difficult or challenging life experiences. These challenges can include trauma or abuse, violence or neglect. Ways resiliency manifests itself are through positive outcomes despite trauma. It includes prevention of trauma recurring even if there is considerable risk. Avoidance of traumatic experiences altogether in light of there being high risk.

To enhance the probability of resiliency in the face of trauma requires support from parents, friends, school, family and the community at large. It's important that a safe environment at home be in place. Trauma itself doesn't create resilience but it can be developed over time with learned skills and support using those skills.

Perseverance is a common theme in God's Word. It's also referred to as endurance, patience, and long-suffering. God grows the personal qualities in us through the process of sanctification. Hebrews points to the example of Jesus as our model of perseverance.

Hebrews 12:1-3 ESV

Therefore, since we are surrounded by so great a cloud of witnesses, let us also lay aside every weight, and sin which clings so closely, and let us run with endurance the race that is set before us, looking to Jesus, the founder and perfecter of our faith, awho for the joy that was set before him endured the cross, despising the shame, and is seated at the right hand of the throne of God.

One can grow stronger through mental and emotional trials utilizing flexibility in response to external and internal demands. Practice lots of deep breathing. Do it often.

Becoming resilient is possible along with finding contentment in the face of trauma. Change your narrative and become your best advocate adapting to difficult, stressful and adverse situations in life.

1 Corinthians 9:24 NIV

Do you not know that in a race all the runners run, but only one gets the prize? Run in such a way as to get the prize. Win!

Experiencing anger, misfortune and trauma can also grow you stronger through resilience. One can experience all the emotions from trials and tribulations and still become resilient and have contentment and happiness in life. Allow God to grow you into resiliency with His Grace and Mercy.

Resiliency is a special gift enabling one to move forward and past all the bad that takes place or has taken place and allows us forward motion. Not forgetfulness or dismissing of wrongs that occurred but courage to go on in spite of traumas and discouragements. If we do not have any resiliency we are stuck in our brokenness. We are forever in bondage to viciousness and atrocities.

It is an insult enough to endure such offenses. Allowing them the final say in your life is doubly cruel. Resiliency helps to move us along however slow or fast we can manage. Forward motion is the preferred direction. Bravery is nothing short of looking ahead at the future and refusing to stare and fixate on the past.

Trauma will always be painful. No one ever asks for it and one cannot prepare for it either. Much of trauma is perpetrated on innocent children. The least equipped to cope and the easiest to harm as they are the most vulnerable, trusting and easily groomed for abuse.

It is always my prayer that God deal harshly with perpetrators and offenders along with murderers and torturers. I'm then reminded that I myself am a murderer having had an abortion. Not because it was what I wanted but because it was what I was emotionally coerced into and believed at the time was my only option.

We must be prepared to find people who were horrible on earth singing in the heavenly choir. We do not have the final say. If that is offensive to your sensibilities remind yourself that Heaven is perfection. No strife, sickness, worries or pain. If you get to Heaven and a mass murderer is there, you aren't going to care. Heaven does not contain worry.

Psalm 25:15 NIV

My eyes are ever on the Lord, for only he will release my feet from the snare.

Galatians 6-9 NIV

Let us not become weary in doing good, for at the proper time we will reap a harvest if we do not give up.

Philippians 2:8 NIV

And being found in appearance as a man, he humbled himself by becoming obedient to death, even death on the cross.

We have abundant hope and justification in Christ. It seems impossible to resist the Lord, yet millions reject Him. Be His loving children, praising God for all that He does for us. Love God harder.

Romans 5:1 NIV

And hope does not put us to shame, because God's love has been poured out into our hearts through the Holy Spirit, who has been given to us.

Romans 5:1 NIV

Therefore, since we have been justified through faith, we have peace with God through our Lord Jesus Christ.

꒷RU꒷H C꒰N HUR꒷

T ruth hurts but it isn't hate. Do not get trapped in this vicious verbal war of words. Also, there is no such thing as your interpretation versus mine. Truth stands on its own merits and it does not require an opinion of it. It simply is the truth.

If we do not have illusions then truth would not hurt us. Operating from illusion and hopelessly lost in it, truth becomes a source of discomfort. There is only hurt where there is a false belief. Satan works hard in this area. He even convinces us that it is not important to love everyone or everyone equally. We love people we are in close proximity too and family members but often stop with our love right there. Many times our relationship to love can even become a political issue.

One ongoing political battle is same sex marriage. Romantic love should be occurring between a man and woman which is God ordained. Acceptance of God's truth does not make anyone "homophobic." There is no fear regarding gays, the fear is disregarding God's intentions. The word homophobic is a highly charged word and is mis-stating the truth which is designed to make people "homophobes," who seem hostile and uninformed and backwards in their thinking.

This does not mean anyone of a differing sexual orientation deserves less consideration, respect and love. As Christians we are called to love everyone, not just people who act and think like us. We are to protect and defend those unable to do so for themselves. By doing so, it is a gift to others.

What God says in His Word is not His opinion. It is true. God doesn't make mistakes. If a statement begins with God it's referring to an attribute of God and speaks of His morality. Many things can have truth, only one thing can be truth and that one thing is God.

John 14:6 USCCB

Jesus said to him, "I am the way and the truth and the life. No one comes to the Father except through me."

Hebrews 6:18 ESV

So that by two unchangeable things, in which it is impossible for God to lie, we who have fled for refuge might have strong encouragement to hold fast to hope set before us.

It's impossible for God to lie.

Scripture has much to tell us about what truth is and points out a direct correlation to God. God is the truth. Truth is generally accepted as love because it is how we were created by God. Every step forward is a step deeper into valuing truth and understanding God's Word. Jesus' promises are the fulfillment of the Word. The fulfillment being His death on the cross. The ultimate sacrificial love.

The reason why truth frequently hurts is because it causes us to come to terms with something unpleasant. Truth often exposes something painful we were avoiding or had no knowledge of.it may require we change our narrative and go against a popular myth or support the truth.

If your chosen beliefs are not as a rule based on God's truth, then reality dictates they are like homes built on quicksand, ever sinking, rooted in falsehoods. That becomes a certain quagmire ending in assured disaster.

God wants for our lives to be built on His truth, not a self designed, self driven truth based on any given individual's personal experience. We as Christians are called to be more like Christ, not more how we incision ourselves to be.

We are to soberly and consciously examine our thoughts and motives. Examining them against the truth of God's Word. If we simply reinforce our own ideas and beliefs we are behaving as non-believers, with no accountability to anyone but ourselves.

Our beliefs help to determine our perspective and impact how we ultimately react to crisis, criticisms and how we navigate in our daily lives. With God as our ultimate guide and His Word a blueprint to operate from, we gain surety and confidence in our destination. Our compass is easy to read and our goals divinely planned.

We each get to choose what we believe, watch and listen too.

John 8:31-32 NIV
To the Jews who had believed him, Jesus said, "If you hold to my teaching, you are really my disciples. Then you will know the truth, and the truth will set you free.

We are free to choose. If someone chooses to believe what is untrue with powerful negative undertones that can even lead to death, it is their right. Doing so can spoil everything as it permeates one's world. God's truth is a way to protect us from sin and the ensuing separation from God.

We can line up our beliefs to match God's Word, or we can keep listening to the world and cultivating a false worldly belief system. To change a false belief system is challenging. It entails actively altering and eliminating thought patterns that may have been in place for many years. Time, focus and the Holy Spirit can realign your beliefs to reflect what God's truth tells us.

That is our ultimate goal on our Christian journey and life with Christ. Transforming our big beliefs will help to disseminate lots of little false beliefs.

We always have God on our side. We are aided and guided by His Word and love, encouraged through prayer and conversation with

Him. We have nothing to fear as we cannot go wrong earnestly seeking God's truth.

All truth can be attributed to God. Integrity should matter to Christians. Make truth your personal quest. You will be blessed in God's presence on the journey. He is with you always.

Proverbs 28:18 KJV

Whoso walketh uprightly shall be saved: But he that is perverse in his ways shall fall at once.

We should not be so desperate to find stories that bolster our position, that we accept anything that supports our position. We should be people who seek truth no matter what circumstances, citing fake facts is a reflection of your faith. We should not bend the facts as it will not help our cause in the end.

1 Corinthians 13:8 NIV

Love never fails. But where there are prophecies, they will cease; where there are tongues, they will be stilled; where there is knowledge, it will pass away.

Psalm 86:15 ESV

But You, O Lord, are a God merciful and gracious, Slow to anger and abundant in lovingkindness and truth.

We have truth readily available to us in God's Holy Word and have no real need to look any further. God's Word is a gift, a blessing and Godly instruction to us in our daily living.

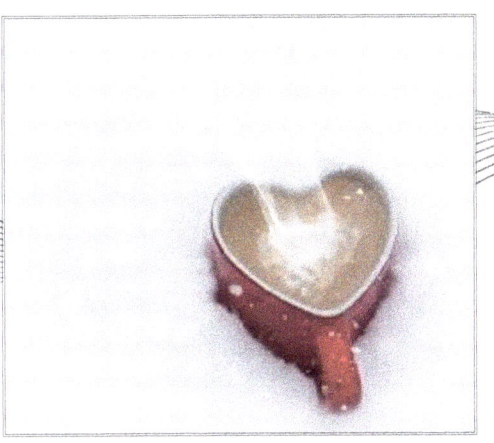

BLESSED BEYOND

To love "beyond measure" is to have profound attachment to and affection for. It is liking or desiring something very much. It is love that surpasses our ability to conceive it. A supernatural love that can only come from God.

God desires for us to have love beyond what we can possibly imagine. More expansive and extensive than what we can calculate. God longs to bless us. We are even loved beyond measure by God. God also intends for us to be blessed beyond measure by His love.

Romans 8:38-39 NIV
For I am convinced that neither death nor life, neither angels nor demons, neither the present nor the future, nor any powers, neither height nor depth, nor anything else in all creation, will be able to separate us from the love of God that is in Christ Jesus our Lord.

To be blessed is to be divinely or supremely favored. When this occurs, it is immediately apparent we are "blessed beyond measure." It's a special gift bestowed by God in order that we have, mercy sprinkled with happiness upon us.

Colossians 3:15-17 ESV

And let the peace of Christ rule in your hearts, to which indeed you were called in one body. And be thankful. Let the word of Christ dwell in you richly, teaching and admonishing one another in all wisdom, singing psalms and hymns and spiritual songs, with thankfulness in your hearts to God. And whatever you do, in word or deed, do everything in the name of the Lord Jesus, giving thanks to God the Father through him.

How are we supposed to respond to the amazing gift of blessings beyond measure? I'm certain many do not even contemplate receiving this special gift. If they do, they probably are not comprehending the amazing gift it is. I certainly had not realized it as a gift nor contemplated who the gift was from in the past. I now know who the gift giver is and can no longer ignore the fact. I celebrate the gifts from God, of which everything flows.

LOVE COMPLETELY

How do we love completely? Does loving someone mean if they are abusive, you need to stay in relationship with them? Does loving someone completely require us to be a victim? It most certainly does not. One of God's Ten Commandments is a call to honor our father and mother. We can do that and respectfully remove ourselves from their presence if they are toxic or abusive.

"Completely" is an adverb meaning to fill up. It refers to "entirely" or "wholly." Doing something completely also means from the beginning to the end. I love this analogy. There are no gaps or detours in loving completely. It is totally fluid. Remember this at all times and when you are discouraged or depressed, know who loves you in a supernatural way that no one else is capable of.

Loving someone completely entails being selfless, forgiving, loyal and accepting of another's mistakes. Relay love to them daily and be believing in them. Loving someone completely has no conditions attached to it. Being completely in love with someone is energizing and euphoric. You don't mind sacrificing for them and continue to make time for them. You can't wait to be in their presence and have an acceptance of them?

Since love, including deep love, is a choice, you make the decision to keep love alive or not. When you decide to work on communication, trust and emotional security, you are making a choice for love.

The three main characteristics of complete love are passion, intimacy and commitment. Signs you are deeply and completely in love is a feeling of safety, acknowledging differences, listening, easy communication, encouragement, trust, effort, collaboration and compromise. The most significant feeling complete love creates is inspiration. It makes you feel as if you can accomplish anything, anywhere and at any time.

Complete love is genuinely the best feeling ever. This is exactly how God loves us. Completely. God's love is unconditional, unending and unmistakable. I can't imagine needing anything more than that. God's love encompasses all our personal needs.

False love is when someone chooses to pursue love for financial or personal gain and rejects a loving relationship with another. It is difficult to maintain false love because there are no genuine feelings.

Jude 1:21 KJV

Keep yourselves in God's love as you wait for the mercy of our Lord Jesus Christ to bring you to eternal life.

Psalm 36:7 ESV

"How precious is your steadfast love, O God! The children of mankind take refuge in the shadow of your wings."

Psalm 109:26 NIV

Help me, LORD my God; save me according to your unfailing love.

1 John 4:7 NIV

Dear friends, let us love one another, for love comes from God. Everyone who loves has been born of God and knows God.

God's ultimate display of His love for us was the sacrificial death on the cross of His only Son so that we could be made free from the bondage of our sin. He left His throne in heaven to live among people who ultimately rejected Him and betrayed Him. There is no greater example of God's love for us.

Love One Another

L ove God. Love one another. These are God's greatest commands. Are we there yet? Are you there?

We never arrive at a perfect place or doing perfect things because we're all sinners. We can however submit to the process and God who is doing a great work in you can begin His plan for your life. It starts as simple as just saying yes to God's request for you. The request is to become a servant of Christ. Listening to Him and doing as He calls. There is no higher calling than to love.

We must prayerfully be open and willing to do as God sees fit for us. Embracing love all along the way.

Matthew 4:19 NIV

"Come, follow me," Jesus said, "and I will send you out to fish for people."

Allow Jesus to use you and to be the reason someone commits to Christ. It is our calling and God's desire that we love others and serve them. Doing for people without expectations. There is no love without service. Jesus came to serve others as a living example.

Mark 10:45 NIV

For even the Son of Man did not come to be served, but to serve, and to give his life as a ransom for many.

Loving one another completes the law.

Romans 13:8-9 NIV

Let no debt remain outstanding, except the continuing debt to love one another, for whoever loves others has fulfilled the law. The commandments, "You shall not commit adultery," "You shall not murder," "You shall not steal," "You shall not covet,"[a] and whatever other command there may be, are summed up in this one command: "Love your neighbor as yourself.

Our love towards others should reflect our love for Jesus. If we truly love one another then we should always be giving our very best, as Jesus gave to us. By showing love to others our love becomes evidence of Christ's love in us for the world to see.

Ways to show God's love to others:

*Listen
*Be generous
*Be encouraging
*Acts of kindness
*Pray for others
*Reflect God's love to everyone

It is possible to show God's love to everyone you encounter either for a moment or for a lifetime. God loves all of His people and so can you. EVERYONE is someone who God loves and cherishes. Jesus died for everyone, even difficult people. He died for everyone out of pure sacrificial love.

When we show that kind of love to others we are mirroring God's love in the world. God's love is actually shining through you. We are just conduits for God's love to get to others.

1 Corinthians 13:13 NIV

And now these three remain: faith, hope and love. But the greatest of these is love.

1 John 4:16 NIV

And so we know and rely on the love God has for us.

God is love. Whoever lives in love lives in God, and God in them.

God's love, care, concern and compassion are new for us every day. God's love is so vast it will never run out or leave us. His love for us yesterday is the same today. Your circumstances can change but the love of God never will.

I can't imagine anything more comforting, unconditional and uncomplicated.

1 John 4:9-10 ESV

In this the love of God was made manifest among us, that God sent his only Son into the world, so that we might live through him. In this is love, not that we have loved God but that he loved us and sent his Son to be the propitiation for our sins.

God's love for us is gentle, faithful, merciful, unfathomable, forgiving, full of grace, with us always even in our suffering, eternal and protective. I don't know if you are convinced but I am awe struck by the depth and commitment of God's love.

One of These Things is Not Like the Others

G OD OR SATAN? Satan often masquerades as God. Safety from the enemy comes from staying grounded in God's Word. Freedom to choose whom we love is a fundamental privilege and right. That does not mean we always put the amount of care and thought into the process that we should. Our decisions can be clouded by our personal experiences. Many problems in our thinking occur as a result of damage or trauma that takes place in our childhoods.

It is during those traumatic experiences that our freedom to choose is replaced with trauma responses and behaviors. Satan has a field day with this inability to properly focus and make wise choices accordingly. This is highly problematic. We end up making undesirable choices based on faulty thinking or little thought goes into making decisions and emotions make the decisions on our behalf.

In this sinful condition we make many mistakes. Clinging to a relationship with God and His Word can help us with. Making our way to better choices, because we then begin to understand God's love for us and His expectations for our lives.

To love is sacrificial in itself. We are by nature poor miserable beggars before Christ. Left on our own without laws in place we would all be in serious danger. We're stubborn, willful and we want our own way, yesterday.

Romans 5:8 NIV
But God demonstrates his own love for us in this: While we were still sinners, Christ died for us.

Ephesians 5:1-2 NIV
Follow God's example, therefore, as dearly loved children and walk in the way of love, just as Christ loved us and gave himself up for us as a fragrant offering and sacrifice to God.

Romans 5:8 NIV
But God demonstrates his own love for us in this: While we were still sinners, Christ died for us.

Ephesians 5:1-2 ESV
Therefore be imitators of God, as beloved children. And walk in love, as Christ loved us and gave himself up for us, a fragrant offering and sacrifice to God.

Hate is often paraded before us disguised as love. We are being indoctrinated and trained to embrace evil and corruption in the world. Not doing so causes punishment by certain groups with agendas if we do not follow or embrace their particular perversions. What has happened? What is going on? What is looming in the future for God fearing Christians? Perpetual sin.

As Christians we are called to love everyone, even those we are in disagreement with or don't like. We love the sinner but hate the sin. Unfortunately a trend is emerging that is a genuine challenge for many Christians. The dreaded word "acceptance." We can love people we do not agree with but expecting us to "accept" any and everything is more challenging as it often takes God out of the equation. God does not expect us to accept sinfulness.

That is precisely where the enemy draws lines. He reduces the argument to accept or reject him or accept or reject God. Some are willing to draw that line in the sand and not cross it or waiver in their position. This often creates fighting words. Differences become labels called hate. How does one argue against the twisting of God's words in scripture, alluding to a false narrative.

The enemy is doing the happy dance when this confusion and war of words and semantics occurs. The enemy loves it even more when the arguments occur within the church walls. He shouts "victory." For those unschooled or uninformed. Spoiler alert, the battle is already won. Christ is the victor. The victory won belongs to God.

As the mask comes off and the masquerade ceases. You may be having difficulty recognizing the confusion that the enemy bombards people with. Remember God's Word. Stay connected to God's followers and be wise because the enemy is lurking everywhere for us. He has no real power though, so simply remind him of that fact next time he knocks at your door. His place is behind you.

Praise our generous Lord who keeps us safe from the enemy no matter how he comes. The enemy comes disguised to trick us away from Christ's loving arms and eternal protection. How is it that we can be fooled, sucked in and played quite easily? It happens because we open the door. Sin freely opens the door on our behalf. Every time you look at your horoscope. All the times you use God's name in vain, curse/swear, lie, cheat, steal. If you use a Ouija board or you are unforgiving. Doing these things, causes you to open the door and invite Satan into your world. He then becomes your invited guest.

It is that simple and easy to do. So why do we do it? We allow demonic intrusion into our lives and often our homes. This mostly occurs in our weakest moments, Satan lurks to attack us. We counter this by keeping the Holy Spirit close and engaged through prayer. The Holy Spirit will supply the power you need for any situation you find yourself in. We never have to take on and fight demonic spirits on our own. We have the Holy Spirit who intercedes for us in our sinfulness.

Romans 8:2 NIV

Because through Christ Jesus the law of the Spirit who gives life has set you free from the law of sin and death.

When we walk in praise, obedience and intimacy, we live in a fuller relationship of worshipful surrender to God and we are in "the law of the Spirit of Life," in Christ Jesus. This leaves us freed from the law of sin and death.

We sin. We have power in our tongue and it speaks sin daily. Life and death lives in our speech. There is no doubt in that statement. It is precisely why we needed the Savior, Christ.

Colossians 4:6 NIV

Let your conversation be always full of grace, seasoned with salt, so that you may know how to answer everyone.

Psalm 141:3 AMP

Set a guard, O LORD, over my mouth; Keep watch over the door of my lips to keep me from speaking.

We get to choose everyday how we will conduct ourselves. Personally, I fail miserably everyday. Not always by choice, but resulting from bad habits and poor decisions. I confess to being a sinner and seek Christ's forgiveness daily. It is my existence. It is my walk with the Lord. Sin, confession, repentance. Like an old shampoo commercial "rinse and repeat." So the story goes on and on.

LOVE BOMBED

Love bombing is an "attempt" to influence a person by demonstrating affection and attention towards someone with a specific goal in mind. It can be positive or negative.

Love bombing can possibly be a form of abuse and people are warned against it as it's manipulative. It is generally designed to make one feel dependent. Love bombing is rooted in selfishness. This is "loving harder" gone wrong.

It is important as Christians and churches to distance ourselves from the love bombing technique. There is a tendency to love bomb newcomers to Christ or to your church. While the initial attention is welcoming, let's face it, it comes to an end. When it does it leaves in its wake, feelings of abandonment and confusion. People are left wondering what happened? Trying to figure out what they did, when it's in fact it's what you did.

This phenomenon has occurred in the wake of mega churches. There is difficulty connecting in such large crowds. So it becomes necessary to have a welcoming system in place to keep people returning and as such, becoming members. That's not likely to happen if one feels lost in a crowd. Smaller churches have adopted this way of welcoming people in, so that newcomers are properly introduced and have an opportunity to meet the Pastor/Priest one on one. This doesn't happen in a mega church unless a newcomer requests a meeting. Mega churches are likely to have several if not more Pastors to meet this need.

You may be love bombed when attending a new church. You may even be invited to coffee by staff and to upcoming church events. You may get lots of initial attention to get plugged in, only to be left to eventually navigate on your own. Picking people up and then dropping them is manipulative. This is a terrible way to treat others, especially in God's name. It's important to be consistently present for people.

How do we love new people harder? Love bombing isn't the answer. Creating genuine connections is. Having a personal conversation about what's important to you with someone and making them feel heard and understood is abundant giving. Listening intentionally to others is a gift. This behavior requires you utilize certain skills. Love bombing does not, because listening isn't part of the love bombing package.

Loving people harder is respectively sharing yourself and listening and being present for others. How would we feel sharing with God our inner most self and God's response was "gotcha!" In our crazy world, the fact the God listens intently to every word we speak are essential blessed conversations.

That God asks and wants to hear from us is a blessing. He already knows our heart but sincerely wants conversations with us. He wants to hear it all, every word. That is not love bombing, that is love sustaining. We have a God that created us, wants us and more importantly wants to hear from us. God is our friend best too.

Psalm 25:14 CPDV

The Lord is a firmament to those who fear him, and his covenant will be made manifest to them.

Jeremiah 29:11-13 NIV

For I know the plans I have for you," declares the Lord, "plans to prosper you and not to harm you, plans to give you hope and a future.

Then you will call upon me and I will hear you. You will seek me and find me. When you seek me with all your heart.

God truly wants to hear from each of us. He is not only our creator and Father but wants to be our friend. We are not merely love bombed, God consistently loves us every day, every minute and every second. Does anyone else do that for you, who does it willingly without being asked? Who else in your life, listens just because they love you intently?

God doesn't want to be love bombed. Most of us when we first encounter God and give our lives over to Him are walking love bombs. We love bomb everyone out of the euphoria we are feeling. We are possessed with excitement over having a new love. God's eternal love. There is no greater gift of love.

The newness of love eventually wears away and the routine of love takes over and will remain. Love requires work. If you are lazy and unaccountable in your love relationships then they will fail to thrive and possibly die.

When we are embracing our love relationship with God it's important to be studying His Word. Stay involved in corporate worship with others who love God. Stay prayerfully engaged in everyday conversations with God.

Matthew 23:37 NIV "Jerusalem, Jerusalem, you who kill the prophets and stone those sent to you, how often I have longed to gather your children together, as a hen gathers her chicks under her wings, and you were not willing.

Ephesians 5:1-2 ESV
Therefore be imitators of God, as beloved children. And walk in love, as Christ loved us and gave himself up for us, a fragrant offering and sacrifice to God.

1 John 2:6 NKJV
He who says he abides in Him ought himself also to walk just as He walked.

Galatians 2:20 NIV

I have been crucified with Christ and I no longer live, but Christ lives in me. The life I now live in the body, I live by faith in the Son of God, who loved me and gave himself for me.

We are to be working at being more Christ like and we do that with God's help, Grace and Mercy. We need to humble ourselves before our Father God and be able to admit our sins and seek His guidance and forgiveness in all things.

We begin love bombing those around us or those in need. Love bombing is an extreme manipulative example of love. We would do better to love assist. Assist with permission those individuals we see hurting or in need. Assist with their immediate needs. Then offer help for the future by helping them to have a strategy for living that best accommodates their circumstances.

People often get into difficult predicaments because they don't know how to avoid sticky situations or have a significant lack of funds. Sometimes a different person looking in can find new ways of coping and getting support for others. Teaching self sufficiency even when people aren't capable of working, is a tremendous help. New eyes, new perspective and new help can go a long way to be genuinely supportive and helpful.

When teaching self sufficiency, you are also love bombing someone. It's important for children to learn self sufficient strategies. It's also helpful to assist struggling adults. Teaching people real life skills is permanent long lasting and necessary help. It is true love.

Skills for managing life while helping teach others:

1. Teach patience.
2. Teach independence.
3. Teach decision making.
4. Teach care of possessions and home.
5. Teach cleanliness.
6. Teach self education.
7. Teach finances.
8. Teach self reliance.

9. Teach reality.
10. Teach about money.

Listening, is the most unselfish act of love. There is an art to listening. When doing this for a friend, it is most definitely a way to love harder. It is an amazing act of unselfish love.

Everyone fancies themselves as listener but I'm here to say that isn't always true. Most people who listen are convinced they're in a conversation paying close attention while listening. While they may be hearing the words you're saying, they might also be formulating in their head they're own response. It is difficult to be tuned into someone when you're working out your own agenda in your head.

The majority of the time the people who are there to, are most likely fixers and rescuers. These people mean well and genuinely believe they are doing good but fixing and rescuing will always backfire.

It does so because if is selfish not selfless.

A perfect example of fixing and rescuing is a story about a friend who stopped on the freeway to assist a stranded motorist on the side of the road. A young girl had run out of gas. My friend offered to go and get gas for her and return as quickly as possible. He told her to wait inside her car with the doors locked as it was late and dark outside. He promised to return with gas for her car.

He found the nearest service station and purchased a gas can that he filled up. He then returned to the stranded damsel in distress. He drove straight to where the car had been abandoned but the car and driver were no longer there. She had found another quicker solution and even though she was told help was on the way she did not bother with that offer of help when a quicker offer presented itself.

Fixing and rescuing backfired. It did for one reason. The fixer and rescuer wasn't asked for help but stepped in determined to help. People aren't as appreciative of help they didn't seek out for themselves. Unsolicited help is disposable.

There are exceptions to every rule but overall the fixing and rescuing techniques fails most of the time. The truth is that your fixing and rescuing is about you not the person you're intending to help. Your rescuing yourself from feeling uncomfortable about whatever problem someone else has.

When making a point to love bomb another Christian, take these steps.

- Bless, don't curse.
- Walk a mile in their shoes. (Metephoricaly speaking)
- Keep God first and foremost.
- Never be vengeful.

Loving people we hate is possible and is important to do. We do this through practice and prayer. God can make things happen that we cannot manage do to our sinful nature.

yikes

Y ikes is my second favorite word. First being the word crap. Yikes, seems to comfortably sum up life for me, deleting expletives and OMG. It denotes calamity, foreboding and "what the hell" nicely. Instead of being a question, it's an acceptance while holding on tightly.

As hard as I've tried to change, control or manipulate God, He doesn't respond well or at all to any of that. Fortunately for me that actually works in my favor, as I do not possess any super powers to see into the future or around corners.

Proverbs 6:6 NIV

Go to the ant, you sluggard; consider its ways and be wise.

I frequently refer to God as unfair. I'm definitely glad of that fact. If God were a "fair" God, I'd be hopelessly doomed to eternity separated from Him as an unredeemable sinner and a one person horror show in comparison to Christ whom I am supposed to emulate. God, who is much wiser than we are, knew this about us and sacrificed His only

Son to save our hides. The only perfect man conceived, Jesus Christ, became our only hope for Heaven. We are forgiven to fulfill the law.

Christ who was tortured and slain for you and me is difficult to fathom or allow ourselves to truly feel. Maunday Thursday, the day before Good Friday is unmistakably the day to "feel" how undeserving we are of that horrible death on our behalf. Holy Week in its entirety is a journey to the cross. Allowing yourself to "feel" the week in your soul will draw you closer to Christ in His death and resurrection. It is a journey we should become intimate with and experience for ourselves.

Christ's death was as ghastly as scripture tells us. It was also life changing as our destination depended on Christ's brutal death, so that we are now saved. Thinking that through, I cannot imagine anything more horrible than an eternity without God. That is the ultimate horror.

I do not understand unbelief in God. It costs nothing to believe in Christ. "If" there is no God and we are the result of some cosmic joke, we have lost nothing believing in God. If there is a God (most assuredly there is) then not believing in God will cost you everything. Logic alone is on the side of believers if you understand that premise.

I'm a chicken. I'm most comfortable obeying laws, social cues and niceties. I like being ordinary. I don't want to go to jail for any reason. As a rule (and those can be broken) I'm a fairly "nice" not always good person. I got a speeding ticket once and never drive over the speed limit and closely adhere to all the rules of the road. I also instruct everyone I ride in a car with, the rules their breaking. I'm hugely annoying in that capacity. I'm not showing off, I'm showing them how. There's a difference.

In fact I'm sort of a rule expert. I don't mind illuminating others on the rules either. More obnoxiousness. I honestly do it to be helpful not hurtful. We are all given special talents and gifts. One of my gifts is knowing rules. So I share.

I will never share about things I don't know well. I never want to look stupid. Ive been self educated throughout my entire life. It's important for me to learn all I can about topics that interest me. I'm confident in what I know and certain of what I don't know well.

I don't understand why people comment on topics they don't really understand. It's unconscionable to me to even form an option about something you haven't thoroughly investigated. People do though. It is the basis for why I wish opinions would be illegal.

Just because school is over for most adults. Education shouldn't be. Learn and grow your brain. Be smarter everyday. It gives one confidence and creates a real ongoing thirst for knowledge. It doesn't make you a know-it-all, it makes you smart. There is no sin in that.

Educating yourself gives you greater understanding about people too. Self examination accomplishes that also. I'm always working on myself. Either through therapy, reading, talking with others and checking in emotionally. I read and research voraciously. I can't even imagine not doing so.

Being that way has grown me emotionally more confident and created a better life for myself than the one I would have been left with as a trauma victim. I wanted to grow beyond that sad scenario. God provided the desire for more inside my soul. I'm so grateful to God for the desire to learn and the peace God has granted me through His love and Word.

Proverbs 1:7 NIV

The fear of the Lord is the beginning of knowledge, but fools despise wisdom and instruction.

James 1:5 NLT

If you need wisdom, ask our generous God, and he will give it to you. He will not rebuke you for asking.

PLAYED

H ave you ever been played? Taken advantage of, used, cheated, lied too? More than likely your answer is of course, yes. It would be less common for you to answer no. Satan works to "play" us. Especially when it comes to loving harder.

It's often difficult to love some people at all. In those cases we might pray for them but not for ourselves to love them harder. We tell ourselves prayer is all we can manage and we leave the rest to God. I've even asked God to put other people in their lives who can do for them what I am not willing to do, feeling insecure and uncertain.

In truth, everyone is capable on some level to show up and be the person someone else needs in their life at that particular time. No one is testing you for perfection. It is pleasing to God to have willing volunteers who love the Lord and are demonstrating that love to others. That my friends is precisely "Loving Harder."

John 8:44 ESV

You are of your father the devil, and your will is to do your father's desires. He was a murderer from the beginning, and does not stand in the truth, because there is no truth in him. When he lies, he speaks out of his own character, for he is a liar and the father of lies.

We are the sinners "playing" and sinning against God along with others when we don't Love Harder.

2 Corinthians 11:14 ESV

And no wonder, for even Satan disguises himself as an angel of light.

Rescued

Y ou have been rescued! You have been saved from the ravages of sin. Unfortunately we live with the consequences of sin, but the ultimate price has been paid so that in death we are free from everything that plagued us on this earth. That includes eternal freedom in Christ. Have you accepted and claimed this phenomenal gift for yourself? Don't forget it's a free offering of everlasting freedom in Christ. Eternally free.

We have love bestowed upon us beyond what we can fathom. With that love we are to be loving others we encounter in our world. Let's be honest, we can love harder. Loving harder is a deeper, more purposeful love. It is the same love we have from Christ. It is abundant and meant to be a gift to others. We need to consciously pick up that cross on a daily basis as we encounter others. It is our reminder to relate to those people we interact with, utilizing God's love command.

It can be challenging to love everyone equally as we are loved by Christ but we are commanded to do so. We are not perfect and in truth are sinners in desperate need of a Savior. With God's help we can begin the practice of loving everyone we come in contact with during our day.

This does not mean we have to like everything people do, just love them as they are. They are Christ's creation and loved but Him. Each of us is lost without Christ. Left on our own we are helpless and do not possess the ability to save ourselves. We are not skillful enough nor clever enough to accomplish wiping out or own sin. Blotting out our transgressions or forgiving our sins. That job is God's and requires Him who is without sin.

Psalm 82:3-4 NIV

Defend the weak and the fatherless; uphold the cause of the poor and the oppressed.

Rescue the weak and the needy; deliver them from the hand of the wicked. They have taken crafty counsel against thy people, And consulted against thy hidden ones. They have said, Come, and let us cut them off from being a nation; That the name of Israel may be no more in remembrance.

Psalm 37:39 NIV

The salvation of the righteous comes from the Lord; he is their stronghold in time of trouble.

Psalm 91:14-15 NIV

Because he loves me," says the LORD, "I will rescue him; I will protect him, for he acknowledges my name. He will call on me, and I will answer him; I will be with him in trouble, I will deliver him and honor him. Is Healing the Will of God?

I will love God harder, forever.

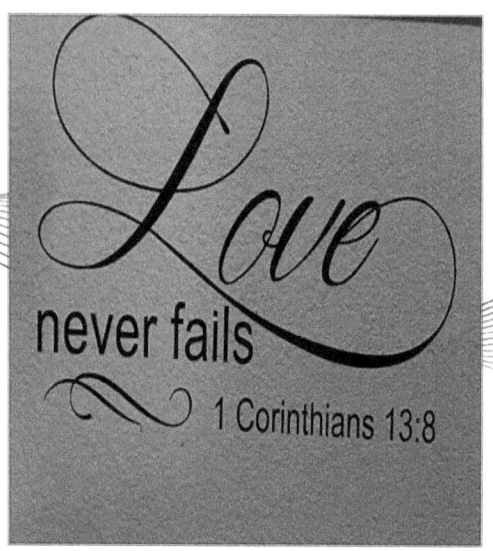

LOVE GOD OUR FATHER

Passion is a powerful word that denotes, intensity, enthusiasm, desire, hunger, craving and a keen interest in something. A passion for God is to love Him with your whole heart, soul, mind and strength.

Psalm 84:2

My soul longs, yes faints for the courts of the Lord; my heart and flesh sing for joy to the living God.

To have passion for God, it is important to get to know Him and understand what He has done for you. To grow in love with God, you must read His Word, where He reveals His nature to us. God's Word is a love letter to us.

Philippians 2:2

Complete my joy by being of the same mind, having the same love, being of full accord and of one mind.

Communication with God is essential to falling in love with Him and gaining passion for Him. We do that with prayer. Our desire to love God will fail without prayer on our journey to know Him.

1 John 4:8

Anyone who does not love does not know God, because God is love.

Another way to gain passion for God is to eliminate the competition. We are tempted to love the world and seek to gratify our fleshly desires. To seek and embrace the world is spiritual adultery. This will lead us away from God and fully becoming a servant of God. If we pursue only Him, He will provide for our needs and desires.

Psalm 37:4-5

He chose our inheritance for us, the pride of Jacob, whom He loved. God has ascended amid shouts of joy, the Lord amid the sounding of trumpets.

Matthew 6:33

But seek first the kingdom and all these things will be given to you as well.

If you are straying in your pursuit of passion for God, backtrack and remember the things you did before. It is not uncommon for relationships to slow or take a dip. Do not neglect to get up and pursue after God again, remembering those things that caused you to grow in love with Him in the first place. The first step in the process might be confession and receiving forgiveness. The result of confession being restored fellowship with God.

Psalm 27:4

One thing have I asked of the Lord, that will I seek after: that I may dwell in the house of the Lord all the days of my life, to gaze upon the beauty of the Lord and to inquire in His temple.

There is no doubt that God will bless the pursuit of passion for Him. It will glorify His name through it. Seek to know Him and grow your passion for Him. A most unique love affair will be discovered along the way.

What does it mean to love God?

1. John 3:18

Little children, let us not love in word or talk but in deed and in truth.

Loving God begins with getting to know and understand Him. That knowledge occurs when we study His Word.

To love God entails worshiping and praising Him. Loving God is putting Him first in our lives. The number one commandment is to love God. That love is undivided love making God our priority, not allowing other things to crowd into our lives.

Luke 4:8

It is written: "Worship the Lord your God and serve Him only."

1 John 2:15

We cannot love this present world and God at the same time.

The love we have for God is manifested in the love we have for others. Loving God is desiring Him and seeking His righteousness, His Word and grace. When we love God's Word, we fall in love with the author and His message to us.

Psalm 42:1

As the deer pants for streams of water, so my soul pants for you, O God.

If you love God, you will obey Him. This however is not merely a matter of following rules and doing good deeds. It's about having God's love written indelibly on our hearts. Naturally we wish to please those we love. When we love God we will desire to please and obey His commands eagerly.

Psalm 40:8

I delight to do your will, O my God: your law is within my heart.

To love God with our soul is to love Him with our innermost being. When we received the Lord in our heart, that is where He came to live in us.

Our soul is made up of our mind and emotions and our will. It is our person, our psychological self. We are to love Him with our whole being.

1 Peter 1:8

Whom having not seen, you love; into whom though not seeing Him at present, yet believing, you exult with joy that is unspeakable and full of glory.

How is it possible to love someone we haven't seen and with our whole soul? Do we even have this ability?

It begins with our heart, the source of all our feelings, thoughts, intentions and our feelings of condemnation or guilt when we have done something wrong.

God purposely created us with a heart so we could love Him wholly and absolutely. However, our hearts are distracted by many things we love and we can find prayer difficult. We must admit that though we can love God, He is not always our first love.

John 4:19

We love because He first loved us.

God first loved us and infused us with love in which we love Him and others. God commanded us to love Him but never expected us to manufacture that love ourselves. God is very aware we are not capable of such love on our own. When God makes a demand, we must realize that He comes to meet that demand for us. Our love for God originates from God Himself.

His is love and He became a man named Jesus Christ. When we receive Jesus, we receive all that He is into our soul.

When our heart is turned away from the Lord by such things as sins, preoccupations and worldly desires, our heart cannot see or reflect the Lord. When we turn our heart to the Lord, we can see the glorious Christ. We see His beauty, His virtues and how wonderful He is. As He imparts what He is and His love for us, our love for Him grows.

2 Corinthians 3:18

But we all with unveiled face,

Passion is a powerful word that denotes, intensity, enthusiasm, desire, hunger, craving and a keen interest in something. A passion for God is to love Him with your whole heart, soul, mind and strength.

Psalm 84:2

My soul longs, yes faints for the courts of the Lord; my heart and flesh sing for joy to the living God.

To have passion for God, it is important to get to know Him and understand what He has done for you. To grow in love with God, you must read His Word, where He reveals His nature to us. God's Word is a love letter to us.

Philippians 2:2

Complete my joy by being of the same mind, having the same love, being of full accord and of one mind.

Communication with God is essential to falling in love with Him and gaining passion for Him. We do that with prayer. Our desire to love God will fail without prayer on our journey to know Him.

1 John 4:8

Anyone who does not love does not know God, because God is love.

Another way to gain passion for God is to eliminate the competition. We are tempted to love the world and seek to gratify our fleshly desires. To seek and embrace the world is spiritual adultery. This will lead us away from God and fully becoming a servant of God. If we pursue only Him, He will provide for our needs and desires.

Psalm 37:4-5

He chose our inheritance for us, the pride of Jacob, whom He loved. God has ascended amid shouts of joy, the Lord amid the sounding of trumpets.

Matthew 6:33

But seek first the kingdom and all these things will be given to you as well.

If you are straying in your pursuit of passion for God, backtrack and remember the things you did before. It is not uncommon for relationships to slow or take a dip. Do not neglect to get up and pursue after God again, remembering those things that caused you to grow in love with Him in the first place. The first step in the process might be confession and receiving forgiveness. The result of confession being restored fellowship with God.

Psalm 27:4

One thing have I asked of the Lord, that will I seek after: that I may dwell in the house of the Lord all the days of my life, to gaze upon the beauty of the Lord and to inquire in His temple.

There is no doubt that God will bless the pursuit of passion for Him. It will glorify His name through it. Seek to know Him and grow your passion for Him. A most unique love affair will be discovered along the way.

What does it mean to love God?

1. John 3:18

Little children, let us not love in word or talk but in deed and in truth.

Loving God begins with getting to know and understand Him. That knowledge occurs when we study His Word.

To love God entails worshiping and praising Him. Loving God is putting Him first in our lives. The number one commandment is to love God. That love is undivided love making God our priority, not allowing other things to crowd into our lives.

Luke 4:8

It is written: "Worship the Lord your God and serve Him only."

1 John 2:15

We cannot love this present world and God at the same time.

The love we have for God is manifested in the love we have for others. Loving God is desiring Him and seeking His righteousness, His Word and grace. When we love God's Word, we fall in love with the author and His message to us.

Psalm 42:1

As the deer pants for streams of water, so my soul pants for you, O God.

If you love God, you will obey Him. This however is not merely a matter of following rules and doing good deeds. It's about having God's love written indelibly on our hearts. Naturally we wish to please those we love. When we love God we will desire to please and obey His commands eagerly.

Psalm 40:8

I delight to do your will, O my God: your law is within my heart.

To love God with our soul is to love Him with our innermost being. When we received the Lord in our heart, that is where He came to live in us.

Our soul is made up of our mind and emotions and our will. It is our person, our psychological self. We are to love Him with our whole being.

1 Peter 1:8

Whom having not seen, you love; into whom though not seeing Him at present, yet believing, you exult with joy that is unspeakable and full of glory.

How is it possible to love someone we haven't seen and with our whole soul? Do we even have this ability?

It begins with our heart, the source of all our feelings, thoughts, intentions and our feelings of condemnation or guilt when we have done something wrong.

God purposely created us with a heart so we could love Him wholly and absolutely. However, our hearts are distracted by many things we love and we can find prayer difficult. We must admit that though we can love God, He is not always our first love.

John 4:19

We love because He first loved us.

God first loved us and infused us with love in which we love Him and others. God commanded us to love Him but never expected us to manufacture that love ourselves. God is very aware we are not capable of such love on our own. When God makes a demand, we must realize that He comes to meet that demand for us. Our love for God originates from God Himself.

His is love and He became a man named Jesus Christ. When we receive Jesus, we receive all that He is into our soul.

When our heart is turned away from the Lord by such things as sins, preoccupations and worldly desires, our heart cannot see or reflect the Lord. When we turn our heart to the Lord, we can see the glorious Christ. We see His beauty, His virtues and how wonderful He is. As He imparts what He is and His love for us, our love for Him grows.

2 Corinthians 3:18

But we all with unveiled face, beholding and reflecting like a mirror the glory of the Lord, are being transformed into the same image, from glory to glory, even as from the Lord Spirit.

We can turn our hearts to the Lord by praying to Him, calling on His name, confessing to Him and spending time in His Word each day.

These simple practices can restore our relationship with the Lord and rekindle our love for Him.

We can turn our heart to Him at any time. He is always there to revive us and bring us back to Himself as our first love.

ᗡHᕬ ᑕᑌᖇᕬ

L ove is the cure for hate and sin. Love from Christ is freely given if we are open to receiving it. Unfortunately we are all living sinful lives in desperate need for the cure.

How do we get the cure? The cure that makes us stronger, wiser and in recognition of our need for it. There is only one cure for the sinful human condition. The love of Christ our Savior. Asking for His forgiveness and help into a growing spiritual life with Him, helps us better navigate the dangerous lifestyle of sin we all live.

We cannot be free from sin at all times but we can be forgiven of our sins and work to do better in the future. Those forgiven sins died on the cross with Christ and His resurrection.

God wants us to cling to Him and seek Him in all things. When I'm in crisis, Gods sacred Words and truth often elude me. I revert to old trauma patterns of behavior. I get hurt, angry, catatonic, retreat and run. It's my trauma response to danger. Discord and harsh words have the same effect on me as the past trauma did.

After I let myself freak out, I give God a try. Sadly God becomes my last resort when I should always approach Him first. A bad habit I'm diligently working at improving upon.

While in general, I'm smart about these things and write about being in relationship with God, there are still times I let my emotions win the battle. Not until I surrender to God do things begin to fall into place according to His will and plan for myself and each of us.

Exodus 15:26 NIV

He said, "If you listen carefully to the Lord your God and do what is right in his eyes, if you pay attention to his commands and keep all his decrees, I will not bring on you any of the diseases I brought on the Egyptians, for I am the Lord, who heals you.

Deuteronomy 32:39 KJV

See now that I, even I, am he, and there is no god with me: I kill, and I make alive; I wound, and I heal: neither is there any that can deliver out of my hand.

Matthew 6:33 KJV

But seek ye first the kingdom of God, and his righteousness; and all these things shall be added unto you.

2 Timothy 4:1-22 KJV

I charge thee therefore before God, and the Lord Jesus Christ, who shall judge the quick and the dead at his appearing and his kingdom; preach the word; be instant in season, out of season; reprove, rebuke, exhort with all longsuffering and doctrine.

If the end is indeed near, does that change the way we should behave in our daily lives? If the end is approaching and we are believers in Christ, we do not need to get wrapped up in all of life's tiny and insignificant minutiae.

For example, you need not ever have road rage when someone cuts you off in traffic. Since you and the other driver will soon die or immediately stand before Christ on the last day. Does it really matter? No. When you get in a fight with your children, family or friends, over a silly issue. Does it really matter? Not in the slightest.

Why would you want to spend precious time working hard to carry a grudge and harbor anger when the end is near? If the end is near, does it make sense to numb yourself and just go through the motions of life? No. Open your eyes; the end is near. The time you have with your family, friends, and neighbors is precious.

Spend ttime blessing people in your life and love them in the name of Christ. Does that matter? Yes. Love harder every day. It matters more than you think.

Be a blessing to people you encounter in your day. Make people feel loved as you rub elbows with them during your week.

Be a contributing reason why someone might choose the light of Christ in their future.

1 John 4:9-21 ESV

In this the love of God was made manifest among us, that God sent his only Son into the world, so that we might live through him. In this is love, not that we have loved God but that he loved us and sent his Son to be the propitiation for our sins. Beloved, if God so loved us, we also ought to love one anothcr. No one has ever seen God; if we love one another, God abides in us and his love is perfected in us.

Love comes in many different shades.between friends and family members, it will never look the same. While we drive to be in love, it can be an easily misunderstood emotion. It is interpreted in many different ways.

Jesus' love for us never changes and is constant and unrelenting. when contemplating the love of Christ for you, remind yourself that it's unconditional. You can sin your way away from Him. You can't talk yourself away from Him. You can't forget yourself away from Him and you certainly can't hide yourself away from Him.

You are His. His creation. Fearfully and wonderfully made. You may not be worthy of God's love but you are worth His love.

Jeremiah 1:5 NIV

"Before I formed you in the womb I knew you,before you were born I set you apart; I appointed you as a prophet to the nations."

Behave in a way you might allow yourself to be a catalyst for love, pointing in the direction of our Lord and Savior. Give love generously and frequently.

Love harder as live has died on the cross for you.

LOVE ONE ANOTHER

Love One Another-John 13:34
Love One Another-John 13:35
Love One Another-John 15:12
Love One Another-John 15:17
Love One Another-Romans 12:10
Love One Another-1 Thess 3:12
Love One Another-1 Peter 1:22
Love One Another-1 John 3:11
Love One Another-1 John 3:23
Love One Another-1 John 4:7
Love One Another-1 John 4:11
Love One Another-1 John 4:12
Love One Another-Ephesians 4:32
Love One Another-1 Peter 4:8
Love One Another-John 13:34
Love One Another-Romans 12:8
Love One Another-2 John 1:5
Love One Another-Leviticus 19:18
Love One Another-Roman's 13:8
Love One Another-1 Thess 4:9
Love One Another-1 Peter 1:22
Love One Another- Ezekiel 16:8
Love One Another-Ephesians 5:28
Love One Another-Colossians

LOVE GOD

Love God-1 John 4:19
Love God-Deuteronomy 6:5
Love God-Deuteronomy 7:9
Love God-Deuteronomy 11:1
Love God-Deuteronomy 13:3
Love God-Joshua 22:5
Love God-Psalm 31:23
Love God-Psalm 97:10
Love God-Psalm 116:1
Love God-Matthew 22:37
Love God-Mark 12:33
Love God-Luke 11:42
Love God-Romans 8:28
Love God:1 Corinthians 8:3
Love God-2 Thessalonians 3:5
Love God-James 2:5
Love God-1 John 3:17
Love God-1 John 4:20
Love God-1 John 5:3
Love God-1 Peter 4:8
Love God-John 14:21
Love God-John 14:23
Love God-1 John 3:9
Love God- Deuteronomy 10:12
Love God-Deuteronomy 11:22
Love God-Deuteronomy 11:13

GODS WORD SPEAKS TRUTH

www.ingramcontent.com/pod-product-compliance
Lightning Source LLC
Chambersburg PA
CBHW051148120626
46547CB00012B/993